Leckie
the education publisher
for Scotland

Higher
BUSINESS MANAGEMENT

For SQA 2019 and beyond

Revision + Practice
2 Books in 1

Contents

Leckie
the education publisher
for Scotland

Higher BUSINESS MANAGEMENT

For SQA 2019 and beyond

Revision Guide

Derek McInally and Anne Ross

About the revision guide

This revision guide is structured around the Higher Business Management course, and breaks down the course content into small manageable sections for you to revise. There are examples of **Sample Examination Questions** together with **Quick Fire Questions** for you to complete with answers from page 124 onwards. Throughout the revision guide you will find **Top Tips** for you to read and take note of.

TOP TIP

The Quick Fire Questions can be done on your own – or better still, get a friend to test you on the different sections.

Higher Business Management

The study of Business Management has become increasingly popular and is recognised as a valuable qualification for most courses in Further and Higher Education. Many students starting to study Higher Business Management will already have completed the National 5 level course (N5). Higher Business Management builds on the skills, knowledge and understanding gained at N5, but it is recognised that for many students this will be a 'crash' subject and Business Management has proved an immensely popular and successful course choice for those needing to get a good grade in a Higher subject.

The content of Higher Business Management demonstrates how large organisations operate and the steps they take to achieve their objectives. The Higher Business Management course is designed to combine theoretical and practical aspects of learning through the use of real-life business contexts.

Studying Higher Business Management will help you understand and make use of business information to interpret and report on a range of large organisations in the private, public and third sectors.

No one comes to Business Management without some knowledge and appreciation of business in society and how it directly impacts upon them as a consumer. The purpose of the course is to deepen that understanding and provide a more mature understanding by introducing the student to common business approaches and theoretical models of best business practice.

The coverage of skills for learning, skills for life and skills for work is illustrated in the table below.

Skill	How it is developed
Literacy	• extended response answers • watching and listening to news reports on business • reading newspaper articles • communicating through presentations/working in groups/discussions/question and answer sessions • self and peer assessment • presenting findings from research in a coherent format
Numeracy	• carrying out calculations, for example when completing a cash budget, financial records and calculating ratios • gathering and interpreting numerical information from a range of sources and presenting it in a table, graph or diagram to aid interpretation
Employability, enterprise and citizenship	• demonstrating an understanding of how businesses work, particularly when looking at working practices, business structures and customer satisfaction • encouraging autonomy/initiative through personal research • developing skills to allow the student to enter the world of work, such as exploring career opportunities • improving ICT skills for a technology-driven society • working with others • using initiative and innovation, and displaying creativity, flexibility and resourcefulness, for example when working in groups • meeting deadlines, being proactive in roles and being part of a team
Thinking skills	• using business vocabulary • using case studies/scenarios • setting concepts in real-life examples • completing personal research and team-working • sharing information and explaining its importance • using information to solve problems • planning, organising and completing tasks

Adapted from SQA Course Support Notes for Higher Business Management

The course builds upon the National 5 Business Management course, which has a focus on small-to-medium size business structures. The Higher focuses on large organisations. The Higher course assumes you will also have a solid understanding of course content at National 5 level.

TOP TIP

Why not buy the Success Guide for National 5 Business Management for some background reading?

Course content – there are 5 areas of study

1. Understanding business

In this area you develop an understanding of how large organisations in the private, public and third sectors operate, make decisions and pursue their strategic goals. You analyse the impact that internal and external environments have on an organisation's activity, and consider the implications of these factors.

2. Management of marketing

In this area you develop an understanding of the importance of effective marketing systems to large organisations. You learn about the extended marketing mix as well as methods of market research and how to keep customers happy.

3. Management of operations

In this area you develop an understanding of inventory management and the methods of production used. You also study methods of quality management and control and the impact of ethical and environmental issues on a business.

4. Management of people

In this area you develop an understanding of the concept of workforce planning as well as complex aspects of training and development, motivation and leadership, employee relations and trade unions and the impact that legislation has on employment.

5. Management of finance

In this area you develop a deeper understanding of the finance function of a business. You learn how to interpret financial statements as well as ratios and budgets.

Underpinning all of these areas of study is the role of technology in managing and running a business and how technology impacts on staff and customers.

Course assessment

Course assessment structure

Assignment (25% of overall marks)	30 marks
Question paper (75% of overall marks)	90 marks
	Total 120 marks

Assignment

This is completed in class and is worth 25% of your overall grade. It is submitted to the SQA for marking. The Assignment gives you the opportunity to:

- select an appropriate business and topic
- collect information from a range of sources that is relevant to your topic
- analyse and evaluate the business information
- solve problems by applying business ideas and concepts relevant to your Assignment
- provide justified conclusions or recommendations for the business
- produce a business report.

The Assignment component will have 30 marks (25% of the total mark). There is a chapter in this revision guide dedicated to the Assignment.

TOP TIP

Start early to gather information on a number of large businesses. This will help you make the final decision of which business and which aspect of the organisation you wish to report on. Keep the details of the businesses in a learning log.

Question paper

This is sat under examination conditions during the SQA exam and will last for **2 hours 45 minutes**.

Section 1	This is worth 30 marks and contains one question. This is a multi-part question that has marks ranging from 1–8. The question is based on stimulus material in the form of a case study that you should read carefully. The questions can come from any of the 5 areas of study and will assess decision making and the application of knowledge and understanding.
Section 2	This is worth 60 marks and contains 4 questions worth 15 marks each. These are multi-part questions that have marks ranging from 1–8. This section samples content from any of the 5 areas of study and assesses the breadth of knowledge and understanding that you have from across the course.

You will be graded in the course assessment from A to D.

Command words

Command words are a common feature of all SQA exams and they vary slightly from course to course. You must be very clear about each of the command words you are being asked in the Business Management exam and make sure you answer accordingly.

Below is a list of command words used in the exam. Your teacher will help you with these words during the course. You must keep practising your responses based on each of them. You should highlight or underline each command word in the question before you start answering.

TOP TIP

Underline or highlight the command word(s) used in questions to ensure that you focus on how you are expected to answer. Take care to make sure that your response to a question is really what is **actually** asked.

Command word	Definition
Compare	Point out similarities and differences between two or more factors. You might also be asked to state a preference. You should try to emphasise or state the unique features of each in comparison to the other(s). **Example – Compare stakeholders' conflict and how stakeholders might resolve such conflict.**
Describe	Provide a detailed factual description. One-word answers for 'descriptions' are never acceptable, you must use a sentence(s). You can describe characteristics and/or features appropriate to the question asked. While examples are not usually credited in Higher Business Management, you may find they help you in a description. You may provide a number of straightforward points or a smaller number of developed points, or a combination of these. Be guided by the number of marks being awarded. **Example – Describe the people, process and physical evidence used by a multinational company you are familiar with.**
Discuss	Examine closely, taking account of strengths and weaknesses in an argument (for and against). This cannot simply be a list – points must be developed. Although negatives and positives should be explored, it is not necessary in all cases. It is important that you carefully read and fully understand the question being asked. Discuss can include the advantages and disadvantages. **Example – Discuss the methods of market research.**

Command word	Definition
Explain	Give a detailed explanation of the impact of some course of action. You must make the relationship clear between action and impact. Give reasons for your points – again, remember that sometimes giving examples can help the examiner understand what you are writing about. You may provide a number of straightforward points of explanation or a smaller number of developed points, or a combination of these – again, be guided by the mark allocation. **Example – Explain the importance of ethical practices in developing positive customer relations.**
Justify	Give a good reason for reasons for what is being asked. **Example – Justify the use of spreadsheets to record financial information.**
Distinguish	Give reasons or explain the differences between two things. **Example – Distinguish between a strategic and a tactical decision.**

TOP TIP

Avoid using bulleted lists with one or two words – it is too easy to miss out on enough detail to be awarded the full marks. Remember that the marks awarded to questions are an indication of the depth of answer being looked for by the examiner.

TOP TIP

Marks will be awarded for the further development of a point, but make sure that you are actually saying something different and not simply rephrasing an existing statement.

Business Management Assignment

The Assignment is worth 30 marks representing 25% of the overall award for Higher Business Management. It takes the form of a report on a business. You choose the business and you decide the topic you would like to investigate.

There is a notional time limit of 8 hours to complete the Assignment. However, you are likely to need additional time to plan and research your study.

The **30 marks** are gained from individual sections of the Assignment. Use these as headings to give structure to your report.

Introduction (2 marks)

In this section, give information on your chosen business and state the topic of the investigation.

To gain marks in this section, identify the business and its purpose. **Make sure it is clear what the business does.**

Provide one piece of relevant information on the organisation and clearly state the topic you plan to investigate. The topic can be from the Nat 5 or Higher Business Management syllabus. Choose a wide area to explore; for example, Customer Care, as broad topics allow for more discussion and are therefore likely to gain more marks.

This is the crucial stage and your whole Assignment will rest on choosing an appropriate business organisation and topic to explore. Try to see the big picture. You will need to find a business in which you can identify problems and in turn offer comments and/or solutions. Do not choose an organisation that is incredibly successful and does not appear to have any issues.

Higher Business Management focuses on large businesses, so choose an enterprise that has a medium-to-large operation. There is no need to be concerned with structure of ownership, although a sole trader might not be able to provide enough sources of information for you to build a report on. It can be any of the following:

- private limited company
- public limited company
- charity
- social enterprise
- local or national government organisation.

An example of an introduction:

My Assignment is on Living Lerwick Ltd. A company established to create a sustainable town centre in Shetland's capital.

Lerwick Town Centre is designated as a Business Improvement District (BID). Living Lerwick Ltd, a company directed by business owners and managers in Lerwick, have responsibility for making the town centre more attractive to visitors and businesses.

During my Assignment I will explore elements of the Marketing Mix.

TOP TIP

You can limit your investigation to the 4 Ps, the Extended Marketing Mix or the 7 Ps. If you decide on the 7 Ps, note you must mention all seven or you will lose the topic mark.

Research (4 marks)

TOP TIP

When using a questionnaire, avoid open ended questions that are difficult to analyse. Give interviewees a range of responses. For example:

Strongly Agree	Agree	Disagree	Strongly Disagree

This allows you to compile percentages.

You are required to use at least two forms of market research and discuss their value to your investigation. **Do not provide any findings in this section.**

Decide on the sources of information you will need to use and how you will collect the information. There is no need to visit the business, but it might be useful to include some personal observations. Most candidates will complete a questionnaire. If you do decide to produce a questionnaire, there is no need to survey more than 10 or so people.

Reference to the research evidence, for example websites or questionnaire, must be provided either in this section or in the appendix. When referencing a book, it is enough to name the Title and the Author.

Explain why you chose the source:

- why the information found would be of use in terms of your report
- the credibility of the source.

Do not simply repeat a list of common phrases like reliable, relevant, up-to-date, objective, accurate, biased, but link it directly to your investigation and say why in this case it was (for example) relevant. Avoid repeating the same advantage for two or more sources as this will gain only one mark. Finally, do not flip advantages; for example, explain why one source is reliable and then describe why another is not reliable. The examiner is looking for four unique values for a minimum of two sources of information.

Here is an example of the Research section:

I used the business website www.tesco.com. I chose this website as it was entirely relevant to my report because it is the business' own website. I used the website to gather details of the wide range of products that Tesco has for sale, to help me identify the extent of their product portfolio. The information was accurate as it is constantly being updated and it gave me prices as well. However, some information about the business could be biased, such as the 'price promise' in order to attract potential customers.

The second research source I used was the BBC news site www.bbc.co.uk/news. I chose this website because it contained information about the economy and effects of recession on business. I gathered statistics and graphs to show the number of businesses that went bankrupt during the last five years. This is relevant to my investigation on 'recession'. I had confidence that the information was from a reliable source as journalists for the BBC have a reputation for being impartial.

The maximum mark allocation for this section is 4 marks. But you should also list the other forms of research carried out to which you later refer in the following sections. This form of research does not need to be justified but must be referenced.

Analysis and interpretation (13 marks)

This section is worth the most marks of any section. Here you will analyse and interpret the research sources and information gathered.

You should report on your findings in relation to the issue you are investigating. Your findings should be in-depth and comprehensive. It would add weight to your findings if different sources supported the same conclusion.

Here are some examples:

From my research (the business website) I found out that:

Pricing strategies used vary from one season of the year to another according to customer demand for certain products. For example, in summer there is more demand for cold drinks and ice-cream, therefore these products were not selected for promotional pricing strategies.

Also:

From my research (survey) I found out that:

60% of customers had complained in the last three months

45% of customers had complained in the last two months

30% of customers had complained in the last month.

This would imply that the business is not meeting their needs and should address the issues they are complaining about quickly, in order to restore customer confidence in the business.

Note that marks are not awarded for simply stating your findings, you must either analyse or interpret your results. You must equally reference your comments to research. It is not enough to simply say the location attracts footfall – prove it with a map.

Here are some other sample phrases you can use to demonstrate that you have analysed and interpreted your findings:

From my research ...

From personal observation I feel ...

I noticed that the business ... this therefore means that ...

It was clear from the pictures/graph/table on the website that ...

From Trip Advisor I found out that customers said ... this suggests that ...

My survey results show that x% of respondents are unhappy ... I believe that the business will have to ...

The article in the newspaper claims that ...

Overall my evidence shows that ...

I am confident that these figures mean that ...

TOP TIP

Avoid the temptation to offer solutions in this section. Keep them for the next part of your report.

Analysis must clearly be linked to the actual business. Avoid general aspects of political, economic, social, technological, environmental and competitive factors (PESTEC). The impact on costs due to a rise in the minimum wage rate will only gain a mark if you clearly demonstrated that the business pays workers the minimum wage.

Conclusions and recommendations (10 marks)

In this section you will gain marks for either providing conclusions or offering recommendations.

The conclusions and recommendation must be based on your evidence and the analysis you have undertaken. These should relate to the overall purpose of the report but also how they might meet the needs of internal or external stakeholders.

There is no need to suggest change. It is possible, with evidence, to conclude that the business should continue to operate the way they are doing.

Sample phrases you might wish to adopt in this section:

From the result of the questionnaire I have come to the conclusion that the business should ...

From the customer feedback I suggest that the business does ...

Summing up my evidence, the conclusions I can make are ...

I would recommend that the business does the following ... this would correct the criticism reported in recent media reports

The business should offer ... this would address the customer concerns identified ...

For example:

Based on the findings from the customer review website, I suggest that the business conduct training for its employees on customer service. This should mean that the number of complaints reduce, and that customers will be happy to return and shop there again.

The course of action that the business should now take is to expand their product range to appeal to an older segment of the market; for example, the 65–75 age group. This will address the lack of sales to customers in this segment of the market as already identified in the questionnaire.

As shown, the spate of product recalls announced in local newspapers damaged the business' reputation. I recommend that the business employs more staff to carry out quality assurance. Quality assurance checks will mean that products leave the factory fit for purpose and there will be no need for product recalls in the future.

Marks are awarded in this section for development points. Marks will be awarded for identifying a cost to a recommendation. If, for example, you suggest more advertising, state that this will result in an increase in the Marketing budget that might initially negatively impact cash flow.

TOP TIP

You should link your Recommendations with the previous sections but there is no need to repeat your findings.

Structure (1 mark)

The Assignment report should be arranged under the following headings:

- Introduction
- Research
- Analysis and interpretation
- Conclusions and recommendations
- Appendix.

There should be no more than four appendices. They can include notes, pictures, tables, graphs, charts, questionnaires, as well as lists of websites, books and articles. Make sure that you reference the appendices so that it is clear what research you are referring to.

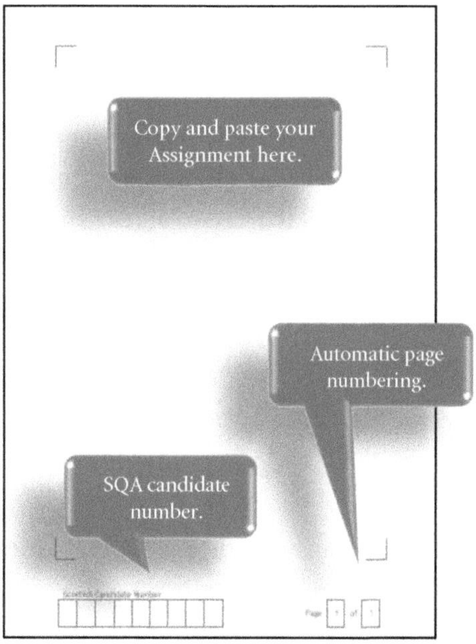

As your Assignment is a business report, it should be word processed. Use a font that is easy to read with 1.5 line spacing.

The Assignment is submitted on an SQA template. This can be found on the SQA website under **Coursework** and **Assignment**.

The report should be approximately 2,000 words. If you exceed this word count by 10% the examiner will deduct a mark. The word count **does not** include appendixes, references and footnotes.

Your word count should be clearly displayed on the front page alongside the title of the report, your name and school/college name.

The role of business in society

The role of business in society

Businesses provide customers with the goods and services that they want and need. Businesses provide these on a regular basis and this keeps the cycle of business activity alive.

Businesses use their resources and their entrepreneurship to ensure that the economy can generate wealth and add value. This all takes place in a fast moving and highly competitive environment.

Business activity

At every stage of the production process, **value** is added and therefore more wealth is created. **Wealth creation** occurs because the good or service is improved during each stage of production, making that item incrementally more valuable.

For example – the production of piece of furniture:

Pieces of chopped trees are passed on to a carpenter who makes the piece of furniture

The carpenter passes the finished piece of furniture to the retailer who then sells to the customer

At each stage, value has been added to the trees that were cut down.

Sectors of industry

Based on the goods produced or services provided, businesses can be grouped into **sectors of industry**.

Sector of industry	Description
Primary	Businesses in this sector extract raw materials from the Earth or the oceans. This includes farming, forestry, mining and fishing.
Secondary	Businesses in this sector are involved in the manufacturing of products. They rely on the raw materials extracted in the primary sector. This includes factories and other processing plants.
Tertiary	Businesses in this sector provide a service. This includes retail, leisure and health.
Quaternary	Businesses in this sector provide a knowledge-based and information service. This includes scientific or technological research and development and education.

Sectors of the economy

Based on who owns, controls and finances a business, they are grouped into different sectors of the economy.

Sector of economy	Description
Public sector	These are organisations that are owned and controlled by the state (government). They can be national, which means controlled from the UK parliament, or local, which means controlled from the Scottish government or local councils. National organisations include the army, navy and RAF. Local organisations include the NHS, schools, housing, parks, theatres, leisure facilities and social work. They provide services that help everyone.
Private sector	These are businesses that are owned and controlled by private individuals. The individuals put up the finance for the business and they share in the profits.
Third sector	These are organisations that include voluntary organisations, charities and social enterprises. They do not specifically aim to make a profit but usually aim to help good causes.

Quick Fire Questions

1. How is wealth created?
2. Describe the four sectors of industry.
3. Describe the three sectors of the economy.

Types of organisations

Private sector business organisations

Public limited companies

A public limited company (plc) is a business that is owned by shareholders who have bought shares (have shared ownership) of a business from the stock market. In return for investing in the business, the shareholder will receive a **dividend** (a percentage share of the profits). Because the number of shareholders can be very large, plcs are managed by a Board of Directors who have been appointed by the shareholders at the Annual General Meeting (AGM).

TOP TIP

Recognise the difference between sectors of industry and sectors of the economy. They are NOT the same thing.

A memorandum of association and articles of association must be produced and the plc must be government-registered as laid down in the Companies Act.

Advantages	Disadvantages
There is limited liability for shareholders.	The annual company accounts have to be published.
More sources of finance are available including debentures.	The shares can be purchased by anyone leaving the company vulnerable to a takeover.
Because of their size, they can take advantage of economies of scale.	The company has to adhere to the rules and regulations of the Companies Act.
Their size can sometimes allow them to have more power in the market.	There are significant start-up costs, which could impact on profits.

TOP TIP

Do not become confused about the words stakeholder and shareholder. A stakeholder is anyone who is interest in the continued success of the business. This includes shareholders. Shareholders are individuals who own shares in a business and therefore are part owners.

TOP TIP

Do not confuse public limited company (plcs) with public sector organisations. Plcs are private sector companies.

Franchises

A person who starts a business and provides a product or service in the name of another business is known as a **franchisee** and operates a business known as a **franchise**. The owner of the original idea who allows others to use it is known as the **franchisor**.

Advantages	Disadvantages
The franchisee is able to start a business with an established reputation and access to business experience.	The franchisee pays the franchisor.
Good ideas will be shared between all franchisees.	If one franchisee creates a bad reputation then it could impact on the whole franchise.
Growth in franchises can result in economies of scale, e.g. purchasing, transport or advertising, and even dominance of the market.	The franchisee is bound to constraints imposed by the franchisor.

Multinationals

A multinational is a business that operates in more than one country. Multinationals normally have a headquarters in one country known as the 'home' country and the other countries they operate in are known as 'host' countries.

Advantages	Disadvantages
Multinationals increase living standards by creating jobs and greater access to products and services.	Depending upon their size, multinationals can hold a great deal of power. For example, the threat of pulling out of a developing country might result in that country's government giving in to exacting demands by the multinational.
Multinationals pay taxes in the country where they earn profits.	The dominance of large foreign corporations can lead to the closure of smaller local businesses.
Multinationals can learn from other cultures and customs.	Lack of loyalty to the host country can result in multinationals pulling out when conditions change.
There are many examples of multinationals that are committed to corporate social responsibility.	Disreputable multinationals have been accused of damaging the environment in the pursuit of profit.

Quick Fire Questions

1. Describe the features of a public limited company (plc).
2. What is the name given to the share of profit received by shareholders?
3. Give one advantage and one disadvantage of a public limited company (plc).
4. Give five examples of franchises.
5. What is a multinational company?

Sample Examination Questions

1. Describe advantages of operating as a franchise. **3 marks**
2. Describe the main characteristics of a multinational corporation. **4 marks**
3. Discuss advantages and disadvantages to the host country of supporting a large foreign multinational. **3 marks**

Public sector organisations

Public sector organisations provide services to the public and are collectively owned by everyone in a country. They are controlled by the government, who will set out their priorities. Finance for public sector organisations comes mainly from taxation.

Central government	• Central government controls and provides people with essential services, such as health and defence. • The Scottish government is an example of central government. Candidates are elected (voted in) to become Members of Scottish Parliament (MSPs) or politicians. • Politicians control central government.
Local government	• Local government is made up of 32 local councils, each responsible for providing services in their area. Local governments have responsibility for things like schools, roads, council housing and leisure faculties in their area. They sometimes charge for using certain facilities (e.g. swimming pools) and this, together with money direct from central government and local taxpayers, funds local government. • Elected politicians control local government and appoint managers to run the services.
Public corporation 	• Public corporations provide goods and services to the public and are owned by everyone in the country. They are sometimes referred to as **nationalised** industries. The BBC is an example of a public corporation. These organisations are funded by money from the government as well as money from the public, e.g. TV Licence fees. • A chairperson and board of directors manage the organisation.

Third sector organisations

Third sector organisations are sometimes referred to as **non-profit-making** organisations and are set up to support a particular cause or activity.

Voluntary organisations	• Voluntary organisations are managed and run by volunteers, who are willing to give up their time for no financial gain, usually because they have an interest in the organisation. • They are controlled by committees, who are usually appointed by the members of the organisation.

	• Funding is usually from membership fees but can also be given by local or central government, lottery funding or donations from the public. • They include the Scouts, Girl Guides or school football teams.
Charities	• Charities exist for the purpose of helping a particular cause, and usually consist of a mix of paid and voluntary workers. • They are regulated by the government who hold a register of all charities. Funding is from local or central government allowances, lottery grants and donations from public sector organisations or individual members of the public. • Charities are controlled by a Board of Trustees. • They include Oxfam, Save the Children and small local charities.
Social enterprises 	• Social enterprises have a main social or environmental aim rather than to make a profit for the owner, but – importantly – are run in a business-like way. • They provide a good or service to generate revenue for the benefit or the cause they represent, and are required to give at least half of the funds they raise to the cause they support. • People who work for social enterprises are usually paid employees but, depending upon the nature of the enterprise, they can often provide training opportunities or work experience for those they are trying to help. • They include the *Big Issue* or the Homeless World Cup.

TOP TIP

Do not get confused with social enterprise and corporate social responsibly. A social enterprise is a third sector organisation that operates for the benefit of others. Many businesses – while pursuing profit or other goals – will operate in a socially responsible way to ensure they have a positive impact on society or minimise any negative effect on the environment.

Quick Fire Questions

1. Give an example of a central government service.
2. Give an example of a local government service.
3. Give an example of a public corporation.
4. Compare the aims of a voluntary organisation with that of a charity.
5. Describe how a social enterprise differs from other organisations in the third sector.

Sample Examination Question

Compare features of organisations in the private, public and third sectors of the economy.

6 marks

Objectives

Objectives are targets or aims that the business or organisation has set in order to provide a focus for their employees and customers. Very often the objectives are presented as a Mission Statement that would be very visible on their website and highly publicised to everyone who works in the business or organisation. The Mission Statement usually lets everyone know what has to be done in order to achieve the objectives of the business. Objectives can change as the business environment changes, for example, in difficult times a business may change its mind about trying to grow and instead aim to survive in the meantime.

There are some objectives that are common to businesses and organisations in all sectors; for example, corporate social responsibility.

The table below shows the objectives that are most common depending on which sector the business or organisation operates in. Below the table is also shown the objectives that are common to all businesses and organisations.

TOP TIP

The main requirement at Higher is to justify the reason for a particular objective.

Private sector objectives	Public sector objectives	Third sector objectives
• survive • make a profit • maximise sales • become market leader • keep shareholders happy • meet managerial objectives • growth	• increase services • remain within a budget	• support a cause • make the best use of money collected • inform and evaluate

Common objectives

- **Corporate social responsibility:** the desire to operate in an ethical manner.
- **Positive image:** to establish trust from others in the enterprise.
- **Customer satisfaction:** to ensure continued existence of the business.
- **Satisficing:** this means to compromise, accept the best available because of constraints, e.g. lack of finance can prevent the achievement of an ultimate goal.
- **Managerial:** where the personal objectives of the managers for financial or non-financial rewards may take precedence over those of the business as a whole.

Methods of growth

Method of growth and description	Reasons for using this method	Disadvantages of this method
Organic growth – this happens within a single business by taking on more workers or by opening more branches or increasing the number of products.	This happens naturally as the business becomes more popular and expands its sales and customer base.	If demand for the business products or services starts to fall, the business will have to make employees redundant or close down the new branches.
Horizontal integration – this is when two businesses at the same stage of production become one.	This eliminates competition and gives a larger customer base. It allows the business to take advantage of economies of scale.	Cash will be required to acquire the business and when two businesses come together they may have to make some staff redundant.
Vertical integration – this is where two businesses at different stages of the production process join together. **Backwards vertical integration** is when a business buys over another business that is closer to its suppliers. **Forwards vertical integration** is when the business buys another that is closer to the customer.	**Backwards vertical integration** ensures that the business has close links to its suppliers; for example, when a supermarket buys over farms to ensure they have fresh supplies of fruit and vegetables. **Forwards vertical integration** ensures that the business has suitable outlets to sell its products and services; for example, when a brewery buys over a chain of pubs.	Cash will be required to acquire the new businesses. Due to different management approaches, the expansion may require extensive staff training to ensure that everyone understands the core purpose of the expanded business. There is an increased risk of failure if one part of the business does not perform as expected.
Lateral growth – this is when a business moves into another market in a similar or related field but not in competition with them; for example, a hairdresser taking over a beauty therapist.	This gives the business a larger customer base and spreads the risk by having different products and services.	Cash will be required to acquire the new business. Staff training may be costly and there may be a lack of demand for the new business products or services, leading to possible risk of failure.
Conglomerate/diversification growth – this is when a business moves into another market which has no relation to the existing business, for example, a supermarket merging with a mobile phone business.	This allows the business to grow and spread the risk in case one of the businesses or products fails. It significantly increases customer base.	The business can become difficult to manage if it becomes too big. The business can lack focus if there are too many different products or services to manage.

Ways to achieve growth

Business growth can be achieved in any of the following ways:

- **Mergers/acquisitions and takeovers –** when two businesses agree to join forces to become one large business, this is called a merger. Acquisitions and takeovers happen when a larger business takes over a smaller one. The smaller business does not necessarily have to agree to this happening and the smaller business usually loses its identity.
- **Franchising –** a business can grow by offering individuals the chance of becoming a franchisee. The franchisee puts up the cash to be able to operate under the business name and pays a share of their profits to the original business owner.
- **Multinational growth –** a business can grow by opening branches across the world and becoming a multinational. This allows their products and services to be available to much larger markets.
- **New products and staff –** a business can grow by developing new products and introducing them into the market. With additional advertising, the new products can help to increase sales revenue. Also, by taking on new staff the overall output of the business can grow.

Ways of funding growth

Businesses need to be able to provide funds in order to grow. There are several ways they can do this.

Retained profits – the business can use profits in order to finance further growth. This is instead of profits being distributed to the owners or shareholders.

Divestment – this is when the business sells off one or more of its subsidiary companies to another company.

Deintegration/demerger – this is when two businesses that had previously merged agree to separate again and operate on their own. This allows each business to develop and grow in the way that suits them best.

Asset stripping – in some cases a business will sell some of its assets in order to release funds. The funds can be used to reduce debt or to finance further growth. Asset stripping can also take place when a newly acquired business has its assets sold in order to finance the purchase of the business.

Buy-in – this is when a group of managers from outside the business make an offer to buy the business and then take control and run it themselves. They provide funding for the new business to grow.

Buy-out – this is when a group of managers from within the business combine forces and make an offer to buy the business. The managers then become the new owners and take control and run it themselves.

Outsourcing – this is when the business decides to use the services of another company to carry out a piece of work for them. For example, recruitment is often outsourced to specialist employment agencies. This means that the business can concentrate on other aspects of the business and potentially grow the business.

Quick Fire Questions

1. Explain what business objectives are, and what a mission statement is.
2. Compare differences between the objectives of private, public and third sector organisations.
3. Describe three reasons why a business might want to grow.

Sample Examination Questions

1. Discuss how a single organisation could have conflicting objectives. **2 marks**
2. Describe possible methods of growth for a public limited company. **5 marks**
3. Explain how different methods of growth can lead to increased sales or profits. **5 marks**

External factors

External factors are those that influence a business but which the business has no control over. A business can simply respond to external factors to minimise or capitalise on their impact.

The external factors are easily remembered through the acronym **PESTEC**.

External Factor	Description and impact
Political	This is the influence the government can have on an organisation. • Governments pass laws such as Health and Safety legislation, environmental targets, tax levels or minimum wage rates, which can make it more challenging for businesses to operate as their costs can increase.
Economic	The state of the economy will impact on the success of any organisation. • An economic recession with high unemployment and job insecurity can be a problem for traditional businesses who will experience falling sales. • Businesses that provide 'cheaper' products can find that a recession will result in periods of growth. Consider the rise in discount supermarkets over the past few years.
Social	Changes in the population will result in changes in demand for goods and services. • Fashion and tastes change over time and this will impact on the demand for the output of organisations. • Demographic changes – changes to the population – will result in more demand; for example, for care homes or alternatively, nursery care. 

External Factor	Description and impact
Technological	Emerging technology will continue to impact on the way that businesses carry out commerce. • The rise of e-commerce will put pressure on businesses to adopt this new way of interacting with customers. • Businesses that are unable to invest in new technology might find their customer base moves on to those who can.
Environmental	Global changes to the environment have seen businesses respond differently to these challenges. • Industries involved in the tertiary sector of industry are often hostage to changes in the environment. Consider the impact that a particularly wet summer will have on farming. • Firms who are socially responsible, caring for the environment (for example, through recycling), can find that an added benefit of this action is an increased interest in their product. 
Competition	This is perhaps one of the simplest external factors to appreciate. • When a close competitor lowers prices, improves the product, increases promotion, changes distribution methods, then others are likely to have to follow or lose customers. • When a competitor exits the market after voluntary restructuring, or because of government legislation to limit monopolies, there are opportunities for the rivals to increase their market share.

TOP TIP

External factors can have negative or positive impacts on an organisation.

Quick Fire Questions

1. Give an example of a political factor that could impact on the activities of a business.
2. Suggest an economic factor that can impact on the success of a business.
3. What social changes have there been that will influence demand?
4. Can you think of any changes in technology that change the way businesses operate?
5. How can a business become more socially responsible?

Sample Examination Question

Discuss the impact that political factors can have on an organisation.

4 marks

Government intervention

The global nature of business has resulted in an increased awareness of how government intervention, often in the form of laws, can impact on the way businesses achieve their objectives. Such actions are designed to support the interests of consumers by protecting businesses, and yet prevent such businesses becoming so powerful that they act in ways detrimental to the public good.

Government intervention is an external impact on business, which we have learned is the '**P**' or **p**olitical factor from **PESTEC**, but it is worth considering this influence under two subheadings: Economic policy and Competition policy.

Economic policy

Economic policy is how government institutions influence business activity. It covers the setting of interest rates, controlling inflation and government spending.

Despite being in different countries, many government institutions are connected and work together to globally influence the world economy.

Economic policy		Influence on objectives
Banks across the world have restricted lending following a banking crisis that started with an American bank called Lehman Brothers.	→	Some businesses have found it difficult to secure funds for growth.
Budget problems in many European countries have led the EU to impose austerity packages to curb government spending.	→	This has restricted the ability of businesses to earn money from selling goods and services to the public sector.

Economic policy		Influence on objectives
Government policy is to keep inflation (rises in prices) to a minimum. They have done this through restricting pay deals in the public sector and reducing public spending and borrowing.	→	Less spending has led to a fall in demand for goods and services.
The Bank of England is influential in setting interest rates across other banks. The Bank of England has kept interest rates historically low.	→	Lower interest rates encourage people to spend, not save. This encourages economic growth.
Quantitative easing (QE) is when the government pumps money into the economy.	→	This provides 'new' money, which is passed on, thus stimulating consumer spending and economic growth.
Governments provide state aid if there is a case that such funding is likely to result in the long-term viability of the business.	→	Several industries have been dependent upon state subsidies for their survival.

Economic policies are influenced by the directives of national and international bodies, including the European Parliament, and institutions like the International Monetary Fund, the World Bank, the European Central Bank and the Bank of England.

Competition policy

Competition is generally regarding as **a good thing** across the world as it tends to make businesses more competitive, which benefits consumers.

Competition policy		Influence on objectives
The European Union single market has removed trade barriers between member states.	→	This has opened up markets to many Scottish businesses, increasing sales but equally making them vulnerable to competition from abroad.
Antitrust and cartels are private agreements between businesses that artificially set prices higher than they should be. This practice is against the law and businesses found colluding in this way will be fined and individuals could be sent to prison.	→	Fixing prices artificially high will allow business to earn abnormal profits.
The government has opened up the market in areas that previously might have been a monopoly. This has happened with the energy industry and most recently with postal services.	→	It is argued that this should lead to falling prices for the consumer and business opportunities for entrepreneurs.
Government agencies will investigate takeovers and mergers and can prevent vertical or horizontal growth taking place if the new joint business would be against general public interest.	→	A merger or a takeover can be blocked and this will impact on the growth objective of a business.

The official regulators of competition include the Office of Fair Trading, the UK Competition and Markets Authority (CMA) and the European Union Competition Commission.

TOP TIP

In PESTEC, Economic policy and Competition policy are part of P (Political) and not E (Economic) or C (Competition).

Quick Fire Questions

1. What impact will tighter lending controls by banks have on a business?
2. How does the adoption of an austerity package reduce demand for goods and services?
3. Suggest an impact of low interest rates on the economy.
4. Does QE increase or decrease economic growth?

Sample Examination Question

Discuss the role Competition policy has in achieving business objectives.

4 marks

Internal factors

Internal factors are the things within a business that impact upon its success.
A business has a degree of control over internal factors.

Finance	• The funding necessary for the business to pursue its objectives. • Finance is of interest to businesses as it allows an organisation to purchase resources. Without these resources, it might not be able to compete with competitors and may have to close. • Businesses have a degree of control over finance in that they can try to obtain it from banks, debentures, government funding, share issues or the sale of an unused asset.
Employees	• This refers to the quality and skills of the workforce to ensure that the business succeeds. • Low morale or motivation can lead to poor customer relations impacting on a business' sales and profit levels. • Businesses can directly improve skills by providing on-the-job and off-the-job training.
Management	• Managers might be good or bad, depending upon their degree of training and their own personal qualities. • Poor decisions made by managers will result in bad actions that could, for example, impact on public reputation and sales. • Many organisations recognise the value of mangers and invest heavily in management training programmes and team-building events for their senior personnel. 
Existing technology	• Technology is constantly improving, which can result in businesses falling behind their rivals. • Failure to embrace new ways of selling, such as through social media (known as s-commerce), will impact on a business with access to limited markets and thus fewer sales than those who do. • Businesses have fixed budgets and limited employee skills but they do have the ability to develop new technology by directly seeking additional funds or outsourcing technology to IT specialists.

Corporate culture

Another internal influence on a business is **corporate culture** or **organisational culture**. Corporate culture may be difficult to put your finger on, but never underestimate the profound impact it can have on the success or otherwise of an enterprise. It can perhaps best be described as the prevailing atmosphere or feeling within an organisation as shown by its employees.

Successful businesses have a positive culture and this is shown in the collective grit and determination of the staff to help the organisation achieve its objectives. An organisation where staff work as a team and speak in positive terms about their role, that of their co-workers and their customers is a sign of a healthy culture.

The creation of a positive culture can be a challenge for any management team. There can be no place for mistrust or suspicion. Good communication breaks down barriers between different levels of staff within a hierarchy where all employees feel listened to and valued. Changing to a flatter structure through delayering can lead to a change in culture. The goals of the organisation must be shared, perhaps through a mission statement, and team-building activities will support a sense of belonging. HR departments play a vital part in ensuring the selection of new employees who are open to or share the common principles of the organisation. Culture is visible in many organisations where staff wear similar clothes – this could be a uniform, a suit or even casual wear. What is important is that it is a common form of dress to show common values and standards.

TOP TIP

Corporate culture can be formal or informal. Formal corporate cultures are **created by management**. Informal cultures are **created by the workforce** and can often be regarded with suspicion.

Quick Fire Questions

1. Describe the four internal factors that impact upon the success of a business.
2. What does the term corporate culture mean?
3. Give an example of how corporate culture can be achieved.

Sample Examination Question

Describe factors an organisation should consider when trying to encourage a positive corporate culture.

5 marks

Stakeholders

A stakeholder is anyone who has an interest in the continued survival of the business. The table below provides examples – **it is not exhaustive**. At Higher level, the emphasis is likely to be on *interdependence* and *conflict*.

Stakeholder	Interest	Influence	Impact	Interdependence	Conflict
Owner/ Shareholders	They want a return on investment in the form of dividends.	They vote at AGM on who to appoint to the board of directors.	Panic selling of shares can cause the share price to fall, resulting in lower funds from new share issues.	The shareholders are dependent upon the management to make the most profitable decision for the business.	Shareholders might be interested in quick returns and resist funds being reinvested in the business.
Management	They can look for a certain amount of experience, recognition or a bonus.	They make the strategic and tactical decisions.	Bad decisions will result in bad actions, such as a bad advertising campaign.	A manager is only as good as their team. Poor workers will let a manager down.	The management want the workforce to work hard, but this is not always what employees want.
Employees	They want high wages and good conditions of service.	A helpful employee will result in happy customers.	Happy customers will mean sales and profits.	Employees need to be directed and this is where they need managers.	Employees might want to suit themselves and reduce opening hours – this will conflict with customers.
Customers	They want value for money.	They can decide to take their custom elsewhere.	This could result in the business closing.	Customers rely on the employee to satisfy needs.	Demands of customers for low prices might conflict with the aim of shareholders for high profits.
Government 	Governments want to see most businesses succeed to reduce unemployment – increasing taxes and reducing benefit payments.	They can provide grants or restrict planning permission.	Failure to give a grant or planning permission could result in a business failing to achieve its objective of growth.	Government is elected by the electorate from the local community.	Government representatives often walk a tightrope between the wishes of businesses to grow and local communities who want to restrict noise pollution.

Stakeholder	Interest	Influence	Impact	Interdependence	Conflict
Local community	Businesses lead to general prosperity in a local community and have been shown to reduce crime rates.	They can protest if a business is causing increased road pollution. 	Bad publicity can lead to a fall in sales or withdrawal of government support, leading to financial problems.	The local community needs the support of the government to provide incentives to keep businesses in an area.	The local community sometimes want a status quo to exist, while businesses often look for restructuring; for example, the closure of a factory.
Suppliers	They rely on fellow businesses for their existence.	Suppliers set prices and credit conditions.	Short credit terms can lead to cash flow problems for businesses.	While a customer deals directly with a business, it ultimately relies on that business' ability to get materials from the supplier.	The manager wants to get the cheapest price from the supplier in order to achieve the highest profit, while the supplier in turn wants to earn the highest profit by charging the highest prices.
Pressure groups	While still wanting the business to continue, they might wish to change the way it operates; for example, to become more environmentally friendly.	Pressure groups can lobby governments to put pressure on businesses to change the way they carry out their activities. 	Protesting and raising public awareness of an issue can result in falling share price or sales.	To have any impact on the businesses, they must have the support of the government and/or the local community.	Becoming environmentally responsible can be costly and result in a fall in profits: both are likely to upset shareholders who are looking for a high dividend.

TOP TIP

'Impact' is the stage beyond 'influence'.

Conflict resolution

The final column in the table on the previous two pages provides examples of conflict that can exist between stakeholders. Resolution of such conflict, or disagreement, can be resolved through:

- the stakeholder with the greatest **influence** getting their own way
- the stakeholder with the greatest **impact** getting their way by holding the other side to ransom

- a compromise between the conflicting stakeholders where each side gives in a bit – this recognises **interdependence**
- the involvement of external agencies to negotiate or impose a solution; for example, the Advisory, Conciliation and Arbitration Service (ACAS) or the local Planning Authority.

TOP TIP

Competitors are NOT stakeholders because they do not want the other businesses to succeed.

Quick Fire Questions

1. Suggest stakeholders for an organisation of your choice.
2. Explain the interdependence of two stakeholders.
3. Explain the conflict between two stakeholders.
4. Discuss how the conflict identified above may be resolved.

Internal structures

Organisation charts

An **organisation chart** shows how an organisation is structured. It shows:

- who has overall responsibly for the organisation
- the levels of authority and responsibility
- the lines of communication and chain of command
- the span of control and different relationships between people within the organisation
- where work can be delegated to subordinates.

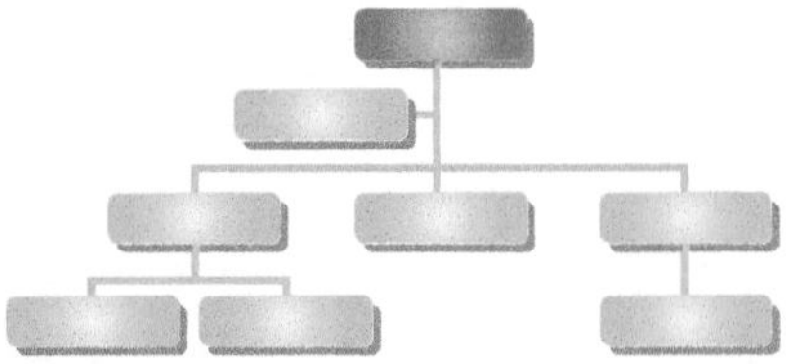

Term	Definition
Span of control	• This relates to the number of subordinates who report to a manager. • A wide span of control can be difficult to manage, but a narrow span of control can be criticised as being over controlling and stifling initiative.
	Wide span of control 
	Narrow span of control 
Chain of command	• The line in which instructions are passed down in an organisation from one level of management to another. • A long chain of command may mean communication and decision-making takes longer, compared to a short chain of command.
Authority	• This is having the power to make decisions within an organisation. • It can denote those whom you have direct management of. • Typically, the higher up the organisation chart, the more authority an individual has.
Responsibility	• This is being answerable for decisions and the actions taken. • This normally refers to those whom a member of staff reports to within an organisation.
Delegation	• This is one of the functions of management and takes place when someone (typically higher up an organisation structure) requests a task to be completed by a subordinate. • This could be because the senior staff member does not have the time, or because the subordinate is more skilled in the task.

Types of organisation structures

Tall 	• These are traditional structures with many layers of management and therefore a long chain of command. • They are sometimes referred to as 'hierarchical' structures. • Instructions and decisions are passed down while information flows down and up. • These structures tend to be found in organisations such as the army or the police force.
Flat 	• Flat structures have fewer layers of management and therefore a short chain of command. • Communication can occur more quickly compared to a hierarchical structure and information can flow around more easily and quickly. • This type of structure tends to be found in smaller organisations; for example, a dentist's surgery.
Matrix 	• Matrix or task-based structures tend to be formed for a specific reason; for example, to work on a particular project or task. • People will come together from various departments within the organisation to form the matrix structure. • When the task or project has been completed, the matrix structure will become obsolete.

Entrepreneurial  **TOP TIP** Make sure you do not get mixed up with the role of the entrepreneur and that of an entrepreneurial organisation structure.	• These are commonly found in smaller organisations, when decisions are made by the owner or manager with very little input from other people – which in turn can demotivate employees. • However, entrepreneurial structures allow for quicker decision making. • It is not a common structure in larger organisations because management would carry too much of a heavy workload. • A good example of an entrepreneurial structure is that of a football manager who makes all strategic decisions during a match.
Centralised 	• This type of structure is associated with a hierarchical structure and decisions are made by those who are skilled at doing so. • Decisions are made by the senior management of a company, with little involvement from staff further down the chain of command. • It allows for a standardised approach across the organisation and avoids any conflicting approaches throughout the organisation.
Decentralised 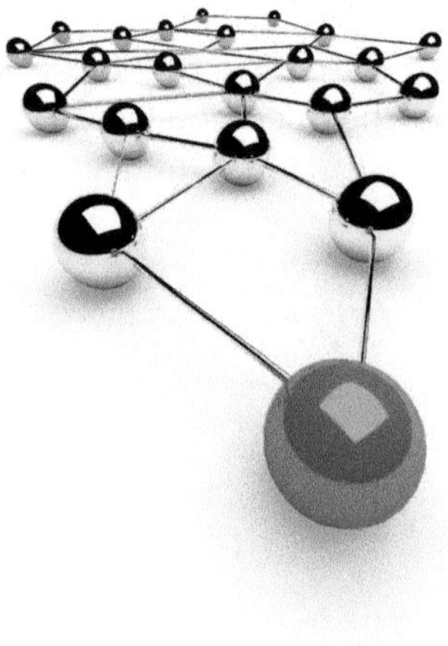	• This type of structure is associated with a flat structure and the advantages that it brings. • This is the opposite of a centralised organisation structure, whereby the authority (the power) to make decisions has been delegated to departments and subordinates further down the chain of command. • Staff become empowered and this in turn will motivate them – provided they want the extra responsibility in the first place!

Grouping of activities

Organisations group their activities in a number of ways depending on several factors:

- the size of the organisation
- the technology used and availability
- the market the organisation targets
- the product, good or service being provided
- the amount of finance available.

<table>
<tr><th>Grouping</th><th>Description</th></tr>
<tr><td>Functional</td><td>

- People working in these departments will have similar tasks.
- The departments that exist will usually be marketing, operations, human resources (people) and finance.

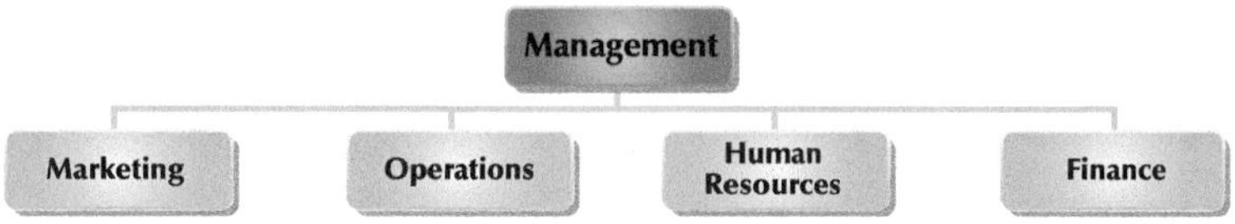

</td></tr>
<tr><td>Product/ service</td><td>

- Each department is based on a different product or service that the organisation sells.
- Each department will concentrate on their specific activity, resulting in an increase in specialist product knowledge.

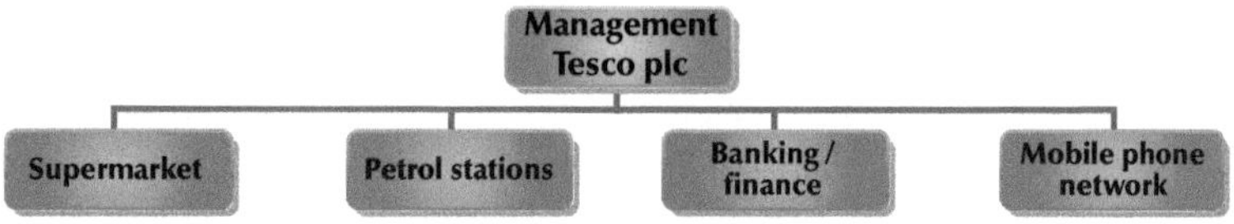

</td></tr>
<tr><td>Customers</td><td>

- Grouping is done by customer types and needs, or by different market segments.
- Goods and services offered can be marketed towards each particular customer group.
- In the diagram below, for a travel company, you can see that activities are grouped according to the customers' type.
- Remember – different types of customers have different needs and wants.

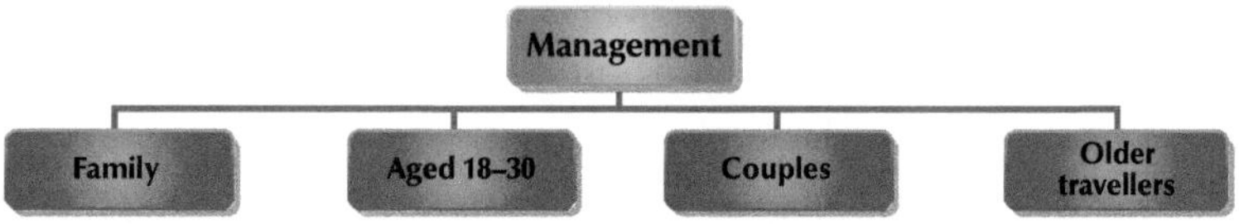

</td></tr>
<tr><td>Place/ territory</td><td>

- People are grouped to focus on a particular area/region.
- This is sometimes known as **place/territory** grouping. The needs of customers within each area can be specifically tailored towards them.
- For example, a Scottish organisation may group its activities by region.

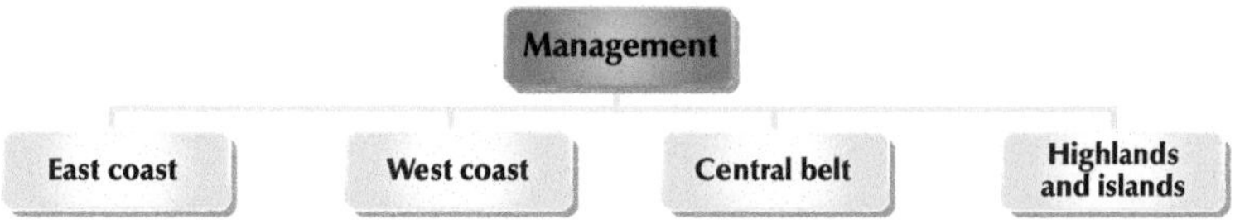

</td></tr>
</table>

TOP TIP

Draw an organisation chart wherever you can on questions to do with grouping of activities and organisation structures.

Grouping	Description
Technology	• A large manufacturing organisation may group its activities according to the production process and technology involved. This often occurs in large organisations with many production processes. • For example, this may include an oil and gas company operating in different sectors.

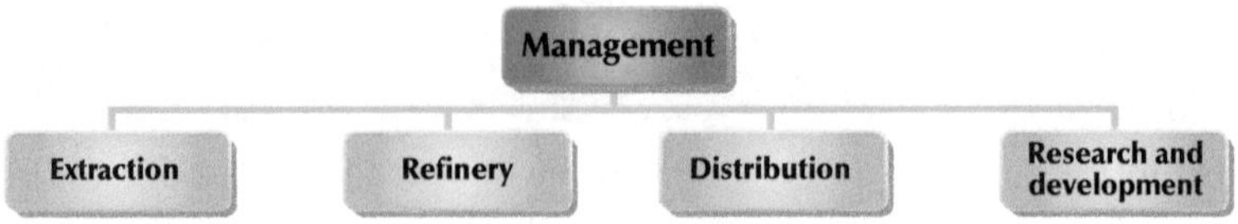

Advantages and disadvantages of organisation structures and groupings

Structure/ grouping	Advantages	Disadvantages
Tall	• Narrow span of control that makes supervision of employees easier • Opportunities for promotion	• Long time to make decisions as chain of command is very long • Jobs are very inflexible as roles are defined in the tall structure
Flat	• Communication is easier and quicker as there are fewer layers to get through • Employees can use their own initiative	• Fewer opportunities for promotion as there are fewer layers • Wide span of control can make it more difficult to supervise employees
Matrix	• Employees are very clear about the job or task to be done • Skills and expertise can be used effectively	• Employees do not always know one another beforehand and this can make relationships difficult • Employees can become too focused on the task or project in hand and lose sight of the business overall

Entrepreneurial	• Allows very quick decisions to be made as they are made by the owner	• Employees rarely have a say in decisions, which can make them feel demotivated
Centralised	• Decisions are made consistently by senior management of the organisation, therefore there is no conflict across the organisation	• Employees are not usually involved in the decision making but have to carry out all the decisions, which can make them feel less motivated or involved
Decentralised	• Decisions are made at department level, which means that employees feel part of the process and are more motivated to carry them out	• There can be a lack of consistency or approach across the business, which can lead to confusion or customers being treated differently by different departments
Functional grouping	• Each functional area will employ experts in their field, therefore the work can be done to a high standard	• It is difficult for employees to move from one functional area of the business to another • There may be a lack of consistency across functional areas
Product/service grouping	• Employees are experts in their product or service and can respond quickly to changes required • Management can identify the strong products or services in the business and build on these strengths	• Employees can become too focused on their product or service and lose sight of the business overall • Lack of consistency between different product or services across the business
Customer grouping	• Employees can concentrate their efforts on the needs of their own particular customers • Customer loyalty can improve if they feel they are being treated well by the business	• Expensive to provide staff for different groups of customers • If there are new products or services introduced, there are no staff to quickly take them on – staff need to be retrained

Place/territory grouping	• Employees can be found on a local basis, which means they are experts in local knowledge; for example, customs and cultures • Customers' needs can be met in the local area, thus improving customer loyalty	• Communication can be difficult across the business due to time and language differences • Each section of the business will need its own support services; for example, administration can be more expensive
Technology grouping	• Employees can become experts in their own technological process, thus, problems can be identified and sorted out quickly	• Expensive to staff with experts • If staff leave, then new staff have to be trained in the technology

TOP TIP

These functional areas will be dealt with later in this revision guide.

Quick Fire Questions

1. What is the difference between a wide and narrow span of control?
2. Describe the terms 'chain of command', 'responsibility', 'delegate' and 'functional grouping'.
3. Explain a benefit of customer grouping.
4. Give an example of how a business might group its activities according to location/geographical grouping.

Sample Examination Questions

1. Describe the effects of increasing a manager's span of control. **5 marks**
2. Discuss the use of customer grouping for an organisation. **4 marks**
3. Compare the use of functional grouping with product grouping. **5 marks**

Changing organisational structures

All of the organisational structures and groupings described are complex and businesses have to make sure that their structure is relevant to their needs. Structures can change over a number of years and for lots of different reasons.

Changing a business structure might be in response to new markets, new premises, new management or lack of skilled work force. Whatever the reasons, the business needs to continually reflect on its structure and whether it is suitable for its needs.

Delayering

Delayering means changing from a tall, or hierarchical, structure to a flat one by removing various levels (layers) of management. Delayering allows for quicker communication, quicker decision making and can allow the organisation to adapt to changing market conditions when necessary. Staff can feel empowered to make their own decisions and use their own initiative, which in turn can increase their motivation and productivity. This is because managers have a wider span of control. Delayering will allow the organisation to save money on the salaries of managers.

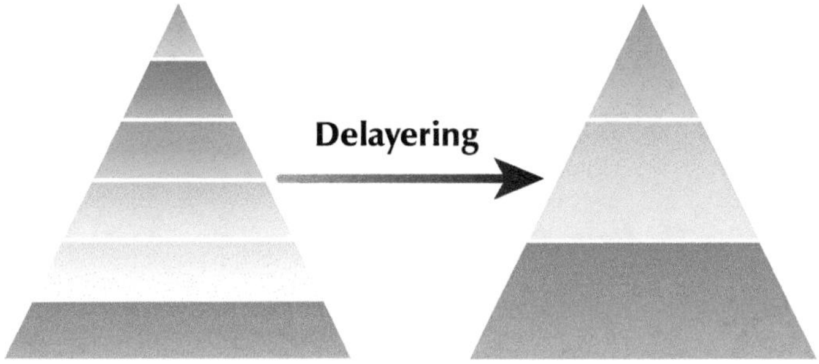

TOP TIP

Delayering does not necessarily mean reducing the number of staff. It simply means that there are fewer layers of management.

Downsizing

A business might decide to downsize in order to keep up with changes. Downsizing involves making the business smaller but there are different ways to do this.

Downsizing might involve removing a section of the business; for example, a specific factory, branch or division (which provides a discontinued product or service). Employees from this section will not be replaced or used elsewhere in the business.

Downsizing might involve reducing the overall scale of production as the demand for the business products has dropped.

Downsizing might involve reducing the number of employees across the business who carry out a variety of different jobs at all levels and in all departments.

The main aim of downsizing is to reduce the overall running costs of business and to make the remaining business more efficient and productive.

As part of downsizing, a business might choose to outsource some of its activities that it feels it no longer needs to support, for example: recruitment, catering, laundry, cleaning. These can be given to other businesses and their services only used when necessary.

Quick Fire Questions

1. Explain the difference between a hierarchical structure and a flat structure.
2. Why would a matrix structure be formed?
3. Where would you tend to find an entrepreneurial structure?
4. What other type of structure is a centralised structure associated with?
5. Describe a decentralised structure.
6. Why would a business decide to restructure?
7. Describe delayering, downsizing and outsourcing.

Sample Examination Questions

1. Compare centralised and de-centralised decision making.
5 marks

2. Describe the main characteristics of an entrepreneurial structure.
3 marks

3. Explain the effects of delayering on an organisation.
4 marks

Decision making

Managers have a significant responsibility in the running of a business through the carrying out of their functional role.

Functional role	Definition
Planning	looking at future needs of the organisation
Organisation	ensuring necessary resources will be available
Commanding	instructing others in what needs to be done
Coordinating	making sure there is joined-up thinking
Controlling	overseeing developments
Delegating	entrusting tasks to others
Motivating	encouraging staff to achieve their potential

Everything a manager does involves making decisions.

Type of decisions	Description
Strategic	• long-term decisions made by senior management • they are broad or general in nature
Tactical	• medium-term decisions made by senior and middle managers • these support strategic decisions and are more specific or detailed
Operational	• everyday decisions that are made by junior managers • these are everyday decisions that are unlikely to have any lasting consequence to the organisation • these are the most numerous in any organisation

TOP TIP

Decision making can be centralised, held in the hands of a few key managers, or decentralised where it is delegated to others.

Factors that affect quality decisions

The quality or effectiveness of decision making will be based on several factors. Not all of these guarantee a good decision, but will reduce the likelihood that bad decisions will be made. These factors include:

- the actual problem that has been identified, and not simply one of the symptoms
- the experience and skills of the managers who make the decision(s)
- the reliability and relevance of the data on which the decision is made
- the amount of time available for information to be gathered and considered
- the resources available (including manpower and finance)
- the commitment of those involved to ensure that decisions are acted on.

SWOT analysis (strengths – weaknesses – opportunities – threats)

SWOT is an **analytical tool** that is used to help in strategic decision making. The process draws together strengths, weaknesses, opportunities and threats, and is used to identify and plan a course of action to support business objectives.

Internal	Strengths	Weaknesses	Present position
External	Opportunities	Threats	Future possibilities

It is most common to set out a SWOT analysis in the form of a matrix. The analysis is broken down into four distinctive areas.

Strengths and weaknesses

- **Strengths** are internal to the business and reflect the current or present position of the organisation. Strengths identify the areas that are going well and might include: a highly qualified management team, large financial reserves, strong market share, or patents and copyrights. They are areas that the business has some control over. Strengths will be used to gain a competitive advantage for the business.
- **Weaknesses** represent issues within an organisation that can cause the business to be vulnerable to competition. These include: out-of-date equipment, an unmotivated workforce and cash-flow problems. Weaknesses are areas that can be improved.

Opportunities and threats

Opportunities and **threats** represent the future position of the business. Because of the external nature of these factors, they are things that the organisation cannot directly control.

- **Opportunities** should be exploited to give the organisation a competitive edge. Examples include: deregulation of the market, developments in technology or lifestyle changes.
- **Threats** are any things that can adversely affect a business and could include potential rises in inflation, recession or potential competition.

Attempts should be made to **match** strengths with opportunities and **convert** weaknesses into strengths.

The creation of a SWOT analysis can be incredibly subjective and so it should be seen as only one analytical tool to be used in coming up with a business proposal. Other methods adopted should include desk and field market research.

Quick Fire Questions

1. Describe the seven functions of management.
2. Compare the three types of decisions made by managers.
3. Describe a factor that will influence the quality or effectiveness of a decision.
4. Give examples of one strength and one weakness that could be identified in a SWOT analysis.

Customers

Every business and organisation needs to know who their customers are and what their needs are. Customers are made up of different groups or segments, with their own particular characteristics and behaviour patterns. The table below shows some possible customer categories.

Category	Description
Age	Customers are often grouped according to age: teenagers have different wants and needs compared with 45–55 year olds. Customers aged 70+ have different needs and wants compared with both of these groups.
Gender	Males and females can have different tastes and spending patterns. This is not being stereotypical – merely stating the obvious.
Income	Customers with high disposable incomes have more to spend on luxury goods and services including holidays, cars and other leisure activities. Those on low incomes will spend more on basics such as food and clothing.
Social class	The jobs that people do are often categorised into different 'social classes'. People in any one particular class may have similar characteristics regarding how they spend their income.
Cultural/religious	Different faith groups may have an impact on spending patterns as well as cultural background, e.g. not eating certain foods.
Geographical location	Where customers live can have an impact on their spending, e.g. in the north of Scotland more is spent on travel than in a city.
Education	Sometimes the level of education attained can influence spending patterns, e.g. customers with a university degree may spend more on travel to different countries.
Family lifestyle	Families are made up of different sizes and patterns, e.g. living with parents is more common until our mid-20s than ever before. This changes how households spend their income.

Consumer behaviour

It is generally accepted that consumers will behave according to the broad categories in the table, so businesses find it easier to target customers for marketing purposes. Consumers want to feel satisfied with their purchases and feel that they have obtained good-quality products at a good price. Increasingly, they are also looking for good customer service and after-sales care.

Consumer behaviour will be affected by other factors too, such as personality, time of year, personal circumstances, family events, and economic factors such as recession and unemployment. Other consumer behaviour is based on routine purchases; for example, bread every day, cat food every week. Often consumers purchase on impulse – they see something they like and buy it without previously planning the purchase. Marketing campaigns and promotional offers also affect consumers.

Product-led and market-led business

- A **product-led business** will concentrate on their product without extensive market research or feedback. They are confident that their product is good quality and will sell, and there is usually no real competition in the market.
- A **market-led business** will concentrate on market research and will update and improve their product based on customers' needs and wants. They are constantly updating to make sure they can stay ahead of the competition and attract customers to their own products.

Quick Fire Questions

1. Describe two customer segments.
2. What factors influence consumer behaviour?

Sample Examination Question

Distinguish between product-led and market-led organisations.

2 marks

Market research

Market research involves gathering information about customers and markets. Market research is essential to the competitiveness of any business and to ensure that they improve their overall effectiveness. Market research is carefully planned and conducted regularly and the results of the research are analysed in order to aid decision making.

How market research information is used by businesses

Market research will usually involve gathering the following information.

- Who are the customers or potential new customers?
- What is their age group/income/location?
- What are their main preferences?
- What price are they willing to pay?
- Who are the competitors?
- What prices are they charging?
- What are the main features of their products and services?

Once this information has been gathered, businesses can use this information in the following ways:

- asking customers their opinions and altering the prices of their products
- asking customers to test out their products and changing the product in some way
- altering the place where the product is sold so that customers have easy access
- launching new advertising campaigns and using new advertising techniques
- offering new incentives and promotions to buy the product; for example, competitions, celebrity endorsement
- targeting brand new markets
- launching a new product in the correct way in order to avoid mistakes.

The main reasons for carrying out market research are to allow the business to increase market share, improve sales and profitability, and to make sure that customers get what they want. Businesses also want to improve their overall image and reputation and encourage customers to return in the future, ensuring customer loyalty. Returning customers will put the business ahead of the competition.

Methods of sampling

In order to carry out field research, a business has to decide on what type of sampling they wish to carry out. Sampling involves selecting a group of consumers to ask questions – but the group must be chosen in some way.

It is impossible to ask questions of the whole population. The type of sampling carried out will depend on different factors:

- the type of product/service
- the location of the business

- what stage the product is at in terms of life cycle
- what other market research information already exists
- resources and budget available to the business.

TOP TIP

When sampling, it is important to get a cross-section of the population so that the results will be more accurate.

Random sampling	This involves selecting groups of consumers at random, e.g. from the electoral register. Anyone can be chosen. This takes time to carry out, but is usually a good representation of the population as a whole.
Quota sampling	This involves selecting groups of the population that meet certain criteria or market segments, e.g. the sample may include 500 men and 500 women. This still gives a cross-section of the population but is not completely random.
Systematic sampling	This involves selecting a section of the population at random and then deciding on the number to be sampled, e.g. choose a starting point and then deciding that every twentieth person will be sampled.
Convenience sampling	This involves taking responses from anyone who is willing to take part in the survey; however, it can be biased if the same people volunteer over and over again.

Justifying the use of sampling methods

Market researchers have to make sure that they use a range of sampling methods in order to protect against issues that can arise:

- bias on the part of the interviewer
- unreliable or inaccurate responses from the interviewee
- errors in analysing the data
- faulty questionnaires
- lack of time available to gather the information.

The wider the range of sampling carried out, the more reliable the information will be in terms of target market. Also, interviewers must be trained to avoid bias, but also to make sure they get the best responses from the public so that the data is as accurate as possible.

Quick Fire Questions

1. Outline three pieces of information that may be gathered during market research and suggest ways in which these pieces of information may be used by a business to improve effectiveness.
2. Outline two drawbacks from sampling.
3. Outline three methods of sampling.
4. What factors determine which method of sampling to be used.

Sample Examination Question

Distinguish between quota sampling and random sampling.

2 marks

Field research methods

Field research involves going out into the marketplace to gather first-hand information. This is called primary information. There are different methods of gathering this first-hand information.

Personal interview, questionnaire, survey	This can be done in different ways, e.g. face-to-face on the street, telephone survey, written questionnaire.
Technology survey	New technology allows customers to give personal feedback on websites or using mobile phones, e.g. online feedback forms or feedback after telephone calls.
Consumer panel or focus group	This is when a group of customers is brought together to discuss a product or service. Their individual responses and opinions are recorded and passed on to the business in order to make decisions.
Hall test	This involves giving a free sample or trial of a product to a group of customers and they are asked to give their opinion once they have tried it out.
Observation	A lot of information can be gathered by observing customers. Observations could take place in a shop, or in the high street. Behaviours can then be analysed.

TOP TIP

Field research is primary information. It is collected first-hand by the business for their own purposes.

Benefits	Costs
The information gathered is relevant and includes personal opinions, which can be difficult to predict otherwise.	In order to obtain meaningful results, large numbers have to be interviewed.
The information is accurate and reliable, as the business knows how and when it was gathered.	It is very time consuming to collect, as it can involve lengthy questionnaires and responses.
The information can be kept private from competitors; therefore, businesses can improve their overall effectiveness in the market.	It is very expensive to carry out as researchers and analysts have to be employed to summarise what the data collected actually means.

Desk research methods

Desk research involves finding out information from existing sources. This is called **secondary information**. It involves using information that has already been gathered. There are different methods of gathering second-hand information.

Government data or statistics	The government publishes information from a variety of sources, e.g. the Census or Family Expenditure Survey.
Printed media, e.g. books, journals, newspapers	These contain information from a variety of sources about consumer behaviour and spending patterns.
Online research	There is a vast amount of data available from business websites, which can be used for market research purposes.

TOP TIP

There is a huge amount of information available on the internet for businesses to access secondhand. However, it is available to all businesses and may not always be relevant.

Benefits	Costs
The information is relatively cheap to obtain or may even be free.	The information may not be relevant to your business.
The information is usually easy to obtain and there is usually a large volume of information available.	The information may not always be accurate or up-to-date or totally reliable.
It is useful for analysing past trends in the market and therefore predicting future trends.	The information is freely available to competitors, so it is not always helpful in gaining a competitive edge.

Quick Fire Questions

1. Outline two methods of field research.
2. Outline two costs and two benefits of field research.
3. Outline two methods of desk research.
4. Give two costs and two benefits of desk research.

Sample Examination Questions

1. Describe four methods of field research. **7 marks**
2. Justify three market research techniques that an organisation could use to assess customer satisfaction. (A different justification should be used each time.) **3 marks**

The marketing mix: product

The marketing mix is often referred to as **the 4Ps**: product, price, place and promotion. Each of the 4Ps is unique in its own way, but the combination of the 4Ps allows a business to develop a marketing strategy that works and that enables products and services to be sold, and therefore profits made. The **extended marketing mix** includes three more Ps – people, process and physical evidence. Each element of the market mix can have an impact on another element. For example, changing the place element of where a product is sold may mean having to reduce the price in order to compete with others. Changing the packaging of a product might give a more luxury appearance and therefore the price of the product can be increased.

TOP TIP

The extended marketing mix includes the 7 Ps: product, price, place, promotion, people, process and physical evidence.

Product

This is the product or service that is being sold by the business. The product will have been developed by the business and marketed to customers.

The product life cycle

Most products go through a recognised cycle during their life. The product life can be short or long, but the stages are the same. The stages of the product life cycle are shown below.

Development	Research and development of the product involves developing a prototype and test marketing in order to get feedback from customers.
Introduction	The product is introduced or launched onto the market.
Growth	Once customers know about the product, sales begin to grow.
Maturity	Everyone who wants the product has already purchased it and sales level out. At this stage, the business may want to introduce extension strategies in order to prolong the life of the product.
Saturation	At the very end of the maturity stage, the product is saturated and no further growth is possible.
Decline	Sales of the product start to fall because there are no new customers.

The product life cycle is shown on the graph below.

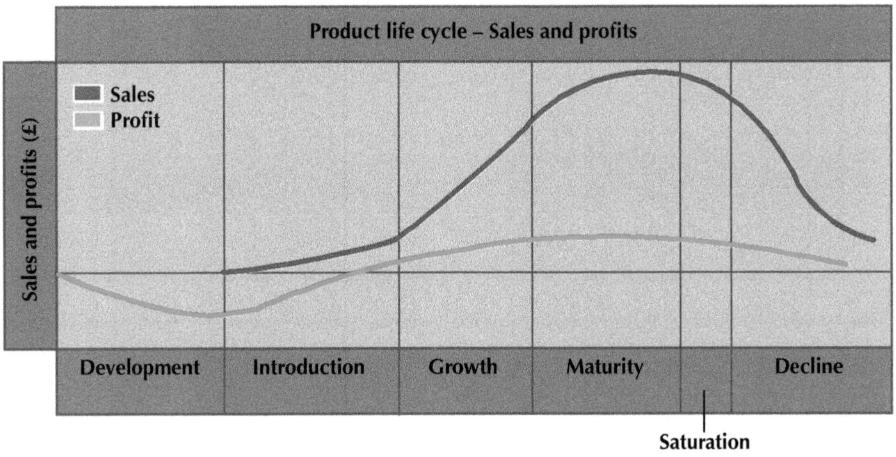

Sales and profits in the product life cycle

During the research and introduction stages of the product, sales and profits are low. There are costs associated with developing and launching the product onto the market. However, as sales begin to rise, profits also begin to rise. At the maturity stage, sales and profits will be at their highest. In order to ensure continued sales and profits, the business has to consider extension strategies. Eventually, as saturation and decline sets in, sales and profits begin to fall until the product is removed from the market.

Extension strategies

In order to revive or prolong the life cycle of a product, the business may wish to use extension strategies. These usually involve changing the 7 Ps in some ways as explained below.

Product	Altering the product in some way, e.g. new packaging, new taste, new flavour, new size or weight of the product. Usually a fairly subtle change so that customers still want the updated version. Or alternatively, finding new markets or uses for existing products.
Price	Altering the price – usually a decrease in the price, but this can be for a limited period to boost demand.
Place	Altering the places where the product can be sold, e.g. introducing online ordering or home delivery or extending into more retailers.
Promotion	Changing the advertising and promotion campaigns to make more customers aware of the product, e.g. new BOGOF offers or celebrity endorsement.
People	For example, training the people who have provided the service to ensure that the customers are happy.
Process	Updating and examining the processes involved in delivery of the service, e.g. having to wait too long for service or attention.
Physical evidence	Ensuring that the physical evidence shows that the service that took place is positive rather than negative.

Extension strategies are shown on the graph below.

Product life cycle – Extension strategies

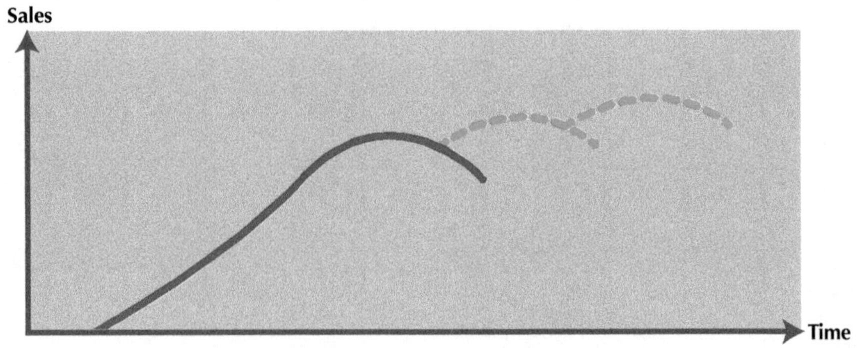

Product line portfolios

Many businesses have more than just one product to sell to customers. They have a range of product lines, known as a **product portfolio**. For example, Ford, Vauxhall and Mazda have more than one car in their ranges, and Cadbury, Nestle and Kellogs all have more than one food product in their ranges to sell to customers too.

> **TOP TIP**
>
> Many large businesses in the food industry are good examples of product line portfolios; for example Heinz, Kellogs, Baxters.

Businesses with a range of products – a product portfolio – will expect to have these products at different stages of the product life cycle. This can mean that as some products are going into decline, other products are being introduced onto the market. Overall, this has the effect of keeping sales and profits at an even level.

The benefits of product line portfolios are weighed up in the table below.

Advantages	Disadvantages
Customers will already know the existing product lines, and therefore new ones can be introduced quickly.	If there is a problem with one product it can affect the reputation of all the products in the line.
Risk of failure is spread across a range of products.	The business may have to invest heavily in machinery and equipment to make a range of different product lines.
Market share can be increased as different products will appeal to different market segments.	The business will continually have to train staff to produce new products in the product line.

Diversified product portfolios

Businesses with a diversified product portfolio have a range of products that are aimed at different market segments. The Virgin Group is a good example, as it provides a range of media services as well as transport and financial products.

The aim of the business is to increase sales and profits over a wide range of products, but also to spread the risks if any one particular product fails. Unilever is another example of a business with a very wide diversification of products. Diversification can be horizontal (when the new products are all at the same stage in the production process) or conglomerate (when the new products are at different stages in the production process).

As you can see from the picture, Unilever provides food products (for example, Cornetto ice-creams) and cleaning products (for example, Surf washing powder).

Analysis of diversified product portfolios

Advantages	Disadvantages
• Selling a variety of products can increase the profits. • It is easier to increase brand awareness. • New products can be launched easily as they will be recognised. • A range of products spreads the risk of failure. • Changes in demand or seasonal demand are easier to cope with. • A wider market can be targeted with different products.	• Advertising costs can be high, as the business has to make sure that all their products are advertised. • It can be expensive to continually research and develop new products to keep a large portfolio. • One product may cause a problem that can affect the whole portfolio.

Boston Matrix

The Boston Matrix is a marketing tool that is used to analyse the performance of product portfolios. If a business has a range of different products, it needs to make sure that continued investment in each different product is worthwhile.

The Boston Matrix looks at the following concepts –

- Market share and market growth
- Four categories of products

The business needs to identify, for each of four different categories of product, whether the product is experiencing high or low market share and high or low market growth. The four product categories are:

Cash Cows: These are products that have low market growth but high market share. They bring in a regular source of income but future opportunities might be limited.

Dogs: These are products that have low market growth and low market share. They do not generate surplus cash and might be worth discontinuing.

Question marks or problem children: These are products that have high market growth but low market share. There might be real opportunities in the future, so this needs to be considered seriously.

Stars: These are products that have high market growth and high market share. They are well established and there are lots of opportunities in the future.

This can be shown on the diagram below:

Boston Matrix

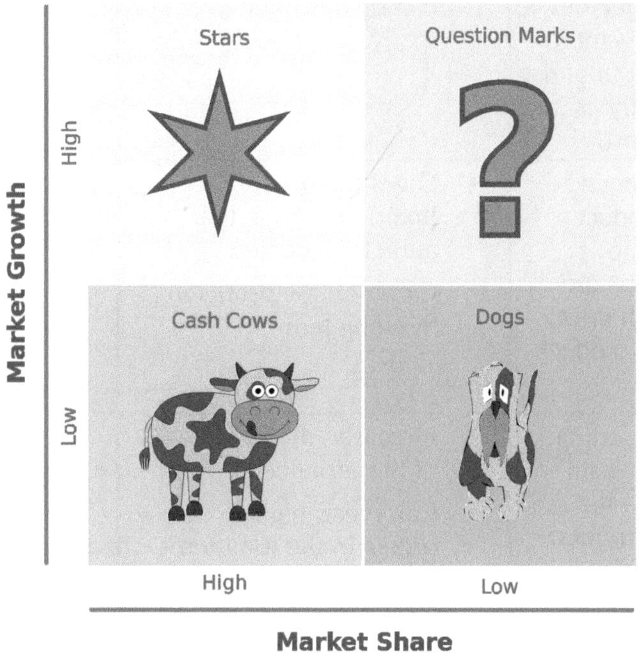

Quick Fire Questions

1. Describe the stages of the product life cycle.
2. Describe two product extension strategies.
3. Explain the term product line portfolio.
4. Give two disadvantages and two benefits of a diversified product portfolio.
5. Give two examples of businesses that offer a diversified product portfolio.

Sample Examination Questions

1. Describe the four main stages of the product life cycle. **4 marks**
2. Describe the effect of each stage on profits. **4 marks**
3. Explain how various methods of extending a product's life cycle can increase sales. **6 marks**

The marketing mix: price

The price of any product is extremely important and extremely sensitive to the demands of the market. There are a number of factors that need to be considered when setting prices for a product.

- What did it cost to make?
- What price are competitors charging?
- Is the product sensitive to very small changes in price?

Businesses usually adopt a pricing strategy based on the above factors. The most common pricing strategies are as follows:

Description of pricing strategy	Advantages	Disadvantages
Cost plus pricing: This is based on the cost of the product to produce. The manufacturer then decides on how much they want to make in terms of profit and adds this on – usually as a percentage of the cost.	• Easy to work out the price to be charged for the product and profits can be calculated easily	• Sometimes the product could have been sold at a higher price due to market demand
Skimming: This is charging a high price for a product that is new and perhaps a bit different. Customers are happy to pay the high price, as they associate the product with prestige or status.	• Gives the product a luxurious image that attracts customers • Can increase profits in the long term	• Can slow down market growth in the long term if consumers won't pay the high prices • Gives competitors the chance to develop products at lower prices
Penetration: This is setting a price low to begin with in order to penetrate the market. Once the product is established, the price will increase.	• Increased market share of the product • Can mean higher profits in the long term	• Can mean lower profits at the beginning • It can be difficult to raise the price in a competitive market
Price discrimination: This is when different prices are charged to different groups of customers for the same product or service	• Can maximise profits as the highest prices can be charged for those who are able to pay • Equalises demand for products that make it easier for the business to cope at busy times	• Customers may object to being charged different prices from others

Description of pricing strategy	Advantages	Disadvantages
Destroyer: This is setting a low price, with the aim of destroying the competition. Once the competition has been destroyed, the business can raise the price again, as there will be no other business supplying the product.	• Eliminates the competition • Increases sales in the short term	• Customers may object when prices are raised again and may go to the competition
Loss leaders: This is when some products are sold at below the market cost in order to attract customers to buy other products.	• Increases sales and profits when the loss leaders are a true attraction for customers • Can attract new groups of customers	• Customers may only be attracted to the loss leader and ignore other products for sale • Loss leaders may sell out quickly, meaning that some customers might miss out
Promotional: This is when products are put on special offer and sold at a reduced price for a limited time.	• Attracts new customers to the product on promotion • Increased sales during the promotional period	• Some customers may only be interested in the promotion and not return • Bargain hunters may reduce the value of the promotion overall
Psychological: Setting a price to elicit an emotional response in the consumer, for example, setting prices at £4.95 or £2.98 (consumers think they are much lower prices than they actually are).	• Customers think they are getting a bargain and might buy more • Increased sales and profits	• Customers might expect this level of pricing all the time, which makes it difficult to increase prices • Customers might think there is something wrong with the products

Use of technology in pricing

Consumers now have access to a wide range of information about prices that enables them to make more informed purchasing decisions. For example, business websites usually include prices of products as well as discounts, offers and promotions available. Consumers can find out this information online before they go shopping.

Price comparision websites such as www.moneysupermarket.com allow consumers to compare prices for a range of products and services to make sure they get the best deal. Price comparison websites are extremely useful for businesses because they are placed in the running for customers to choose from. However, these websites can be complicated and they do not always compare like with like. Regardless, many large companies are now linked to these websites.

TOP TIP

Pricing strategies and decisions are now crucial to the success of a business because competition is so fierce, and customers are much more knowledgeable about the competition.

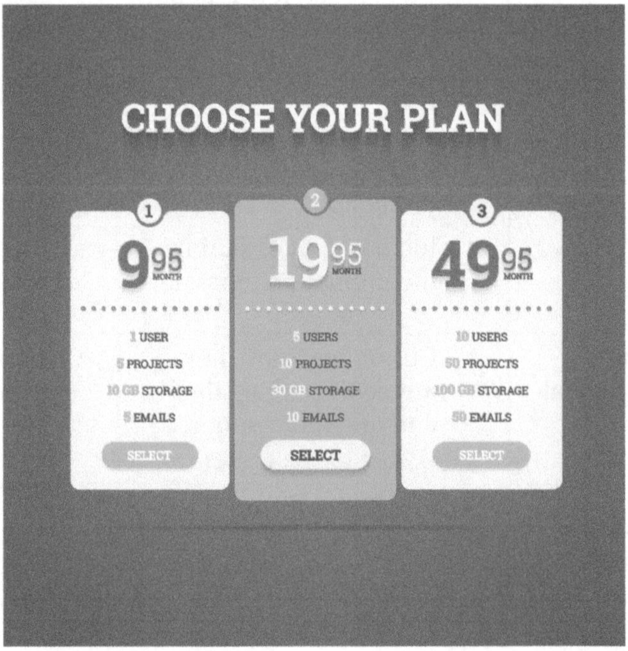

Quick Fire Questions

1. Outline two factors to be taken into account when setting prices.
2. Explain how cost plus pricing works.
3. What is psychological pricing?
4. How do customers use price comparison websites?

Sample Examination Questions

1. Describe two pricing tactics that an organisation could use when selling an exclusive product.

   4 marks

2. Describe three pricing tactics that could be used when an organisation attempts to break into a new market.

   6 marks

The marketing mix: place

The place element of the marketing mix has changed considerably in the last ten years. Place refers to how the product gets to the consumer and where it is sold.

Products get to consumers in a variety of different ways – often referred to as channels of distribution. This means how the product is transported and distributed to the consumer. There are four main channels.

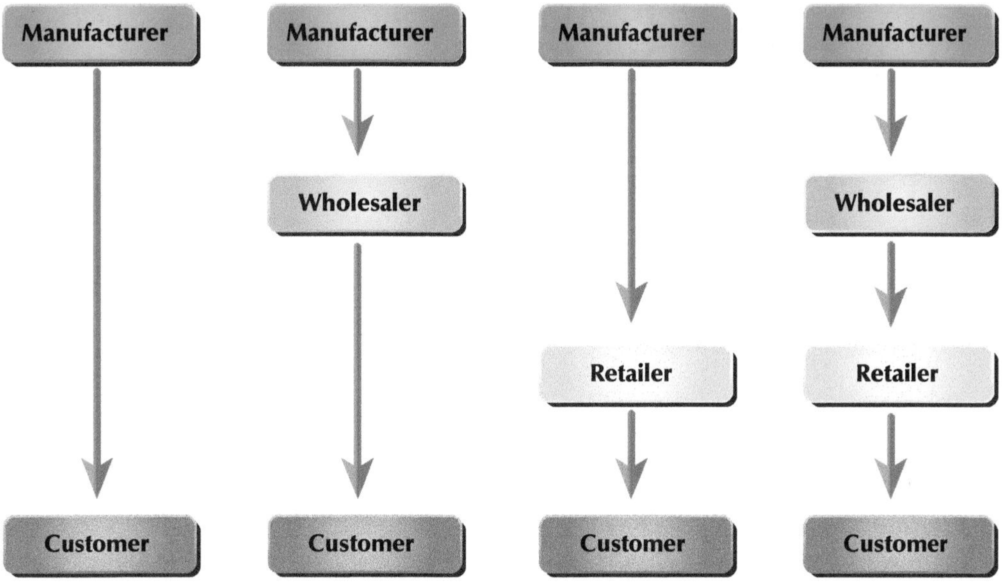

The table below weighs up the benefits of using different types of distribution channels.

Distribution channel	Benefits	Costs
Wholesalers	For the consumer or small business outlet – the bulk is broken down so they can buy in small amounts For the small business – the wholesaler may provide some discounts for buying in bulk	For the consumer – increased prices compared to direct sales For the manufacturer – the wholesaler needs to be reliable, and promote and sell the product in the way they want
Retailers	For the consumer – a local place to buy products and to obtain advice and after-sales service; they can also get finance and delivery for large items For the manufacturer – the retailer provides information and advice, promotion and advertising for the products they wish to get to the consumers; the choice of retailer may contribute to the success overall of the product	For the consumer – sometimes too much choice, or retailers deciding which products they wish to sell rather than what consumers really want For the manufacturer – they have to rely on the retailer promoting and selling the product in the way they want For the manufacturer – deciding on which type of retailer to choose to sell their products can be a problem (e.g. mainstream fashion, aspirational or luxury)

Distribution channel	Benefits	Costs
Direct sales	For the consumer – direct selling usually means a more tailor-made product for their own requirements  For the manufacturer – they can maintain contact with their customers to ensure they provide what they want	For the consumer – there may not be a wide choice, therefore prices can be difficult to negotiate For the manufacturer – they need to employ additional staff to do the selling

The role of the wholesaler and retailer

The **wholesaler i**s often referred to as the 'middleman'. They are the link between the manufacturer and the retailer. The manufacturer needs to get their goods out into the market for customers to buy them as soon as possible. Wholesalers offer this service to the manufacturer. They 'buy up' the finished products from the manufacturer and sell them on to the retailer. Wholesalers buy in bulk, as they have the space to store large quantities of products in the correct conditions. They then break down the 'bulk' and sell to retailers in smaller quantities for them to sell in their shops.

Wholesalers also buy from different manufacturers, so the retailer can have a choice of different products. The wholesaler often gives credit to the retailers to enable them to stock their shops with the range and variety of products that customers want.

The **retailer** is the last link in the chain of distribution. They provide the goods and services that customers want. They enable customers to buy in small quantities from locations that are suitable for them. They provide personal service and contact with the customers. They provide before-sales and after-sales service and advice. They also provide choice.

The retailer also feeds back to the wholesaler on market trends, consumer preferences and demand. The wholesaler can then adjust their stock requirements so that they are not left with unsold stocks in their warehouses.

Types of retailer

There are a wide variety of retailers in the UK today – both on the high street and online. Broadly speaking, they come under the following headings.

- **Independent retailers:** These are usually small shops that sell a very limited range of goods; for example, corner grocery stores, hat shops, fishing supplies and bicycle shops. They are often operated as sole traders.
- **Multiple chain stores:** These are spread over the country and are the same wherever you find them; for example, Marks and Spencer, Top Shop, Office, Homebase, B&Q, Boots and Superdrug. They can sell a wide range of products or specialise in a smaller area. They usually have an online store that provides a delivery service to customers.
- **Supermarkets:** These offer food and non-food products and are well known throughout the country; for example, Tesco, ASDA, Morrisons and Sainsbury's.
- **Department stores:** They are also found throughout the country, but there are fewer of them and they usually stock more specialised and up-market brands; for example, Debenhams, John Lewis and House of Fraser.
- **Franchises:** They are operated by individuals who have purchased the rights to trade under the 'brand name'; for example, McDonald's, The Body Shop and Pizza Hut.
- **Mail order/catalogues:** Most catalogues now provide online shopping services, where customers can place orders for goods to be delivered straight to their homes. Some companies still send out copies of their catalogues for customers to place orders by mail.
- **TV shopping channels:** Many manufacturers offer their products for sale via TV shopping channels; for example, QVC. The channel may specialise in one particular product; for example, jewellery or offer a wide variety of products.

Quick Fire Questions

1. Describe two channels of distribution.
2. Outline two benefits of using wholesalers.
3. Outline two benefits of using retailers.

Sample Examination Questions

1. Describe the reasons why some manufacturers sell their products to retailers rather than directly to customers. **4 marks**
2. Explain the advantages and disadvantages of using a wholesaler. **5 marks**

The marketing mix: promotion

Promotion is aimed at two distinct groups – those who will sell the product (retailers) and those who will buy the product (consumers).

Into the pipeline promotions

These are aimed at retailers who agree to sell the finished products from the manufacturer. There are a number of different promotions:

- **dealer promotions and loaders,** such as prizes given to the retailer that sells the most of the product, or extra products given for volume; for example, one free box of sweets for every five boxes stocked
- **point of sale displays** including posters, stands, free samples
- **staff training** on the product features and advantages so that they can deal confidently with consumers who are purchasing
- **extended credit** given to enable retailers to purchase stock
- **sale or return** where the retailer can return unsold items.

Out of the pipeline promotions

These are aimed at consumers in order to persuade them to buy products. There are a number of different promotions:

- discounts
- special offers – buy one get one free
- free samples or tasting
- price reductions; for example, 65p off for a limited period only
- loyalty cards
- celebrity endorsement
- vouchers or coupons
- free entry into competitions.

These promotions are effective in the short term, as they attract consumers' attention. There is a wide variety of choice for consumers, so the difference between purchasing one product and another may just be the fact that on the day there was a free sample given away, or a price reduction or entry into a competition.

TOP TIP

Promotions are very good for increasing sales in the short term.

Public relations

The way that businesses and organisations are perceived by the public is often managed by proactive 'public relations' (PR). There may be a separate department or section in the business or organisation that deals specifically with PR. Indeed, many celebrities have their own PR assistant who deals exclusively with their public image.

PR involves providing information about products and services – and the business in general – that shows the business in a positive way. This can involve working closely with the marketing and advertising team; and may involve releasing press statements, gaining publicity for making charity donations, engaging celebrities for advertising or product endorsements and sponsoring events such as sports. Most importantly, it can involve damage limitation to the business reputation when things go wrong, such as industrial action, faulty products, accidents in the workplace or bad customer feedback. An effective PR team will anticipate problems before they develop into something that can seriously damage the business' reputation.

Quick Fire Questions

1. Distinguish between 'into the pipeline' and 'out of the pipeline' promotions.

The extended marketing mix

The extended marketing mix

As mentioned at the beginning of this chapter, the marketing mix has now been extended to include the 7 Ps. The three additional Ps are people, process and physical evidence, and they are important in the delivery of services, rather than businesses that provide tangible products.

People

The 'people' part of the extended marketing mix includes employees, managers and customers.

Employees have to be trained appropriately to make sure they have the skills, knowledge and expertise to do their jobs properly and to a high standard. This also includes customer service training if employees are dealing directly with the public. Anyone who comes into contact with customers makes an important impression about the business overall – therefore it has to be positive and impressive. Customers have so much choice today that the employees need to make that vital first impression.

Employees also have to be continually developed in their role by continuous professional development, target setting and appraisal systems. Employees are one of the greatest assets that a business has, but they are also one of the most expensive. Therefore it is worthwhile investing in them.

Managers have to be highly trained in making decisions and using limited resources wisely. They will make decisions at a strategic and tactical level about the overall direction the business is heading in. They must be given the right level of authority and responsibility to let the business be successful, but also challenged if this does not happen. Managers have to develop corporate culture and wellbeing so that employees feel valued and motivated at work.

Managers have to encourage enterprising skills and attitudes in their employees in order to stay competitive. They must be prepared to take risks with research, innovation and new ideas. They need to ensure that market research and customer feedback is acted upon quickly and effectively.

Managers have to set targets for employees that are realistic and achievable. They should provide the appropriate balance of support and encouragement, as well as performance management for employees who are not delivering.

Customers have to be treated with respect and care. Customer service policies must be put into practice and customers must be informed regularly about services on offer. Customers must be offered before-sales and after-sales advice. Customer enquiries should be answered quickly and a variety of options offered. After-sales service in the form of follow-ups, guarantees and refunds are extremely important for customer loyalty and retention.

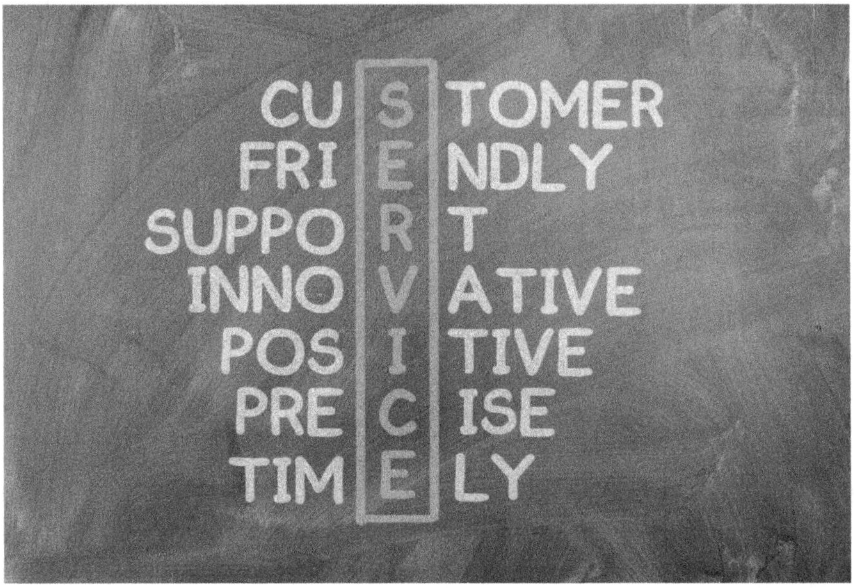

Many businesses and organisations take part in the 'Investors in People' award to demonstrate to their customers the standards of customer care they can expect.

Process

In order to deliver an efficient service there must be 'process' in place so that everyone knows what to do, when to do it and how to do it. For example, when you attend school you are marked present on a register in the classroom. This information is transferred to the school office. If you are absent, the school office contact your parents, and also contact pastoral care. This does not happen by accident. This is a planned process that takes place every day and everyone knows their role.

The process of giving a service is crucial to customer satisfaction. Customers are often in a hurry and do not have time to wait or be offered lengthy explanations or systems that are confusing or time-consuming.

The 'process' of delivering the service to customers has to be robustly tried and tested. If the service is sloppy, slow or inefficient, customers have a choice and will go elsewhere.

There are different processes depending on the services being provided. A small hairdresser will provide very personal contact with the customer as soon as they enter the salon. The customer will expect them to be on time and be offered refreshments if there is any delay. However, a large business providing home or car insurance will have a different process. This could be an application on a website followed up with documents received through the post; or it could be an agent providing a home visit with a quote that is then followed up with the correct documents. Either way, the process has to be accessible for the customer, easy to complete and achieved within an acceptable time period. Customers are put off by lengthy conversations to call centres that involve being passed from one operator to another or pressing numerous buttons to navigate around the system.

Restaurants, bars and cafes involve different processes again. Customers expect food to be served appropriately and within an acceptable time period. Busy restaurants with lengthy waiting times and substandard goods or services will not be tolerated by customers who have a choice.

Physical evidence

The physical evidence relates to where the service is being delivered from. Customers cannot 'see' the service in advance so they need to have confidence that the service will be acceptable. The physical evidence they see takes many different forms.

- **Physical environment:** This can be the physical building as well as the image of employees. Buildings and reception areas should be bright and welcoming for customers. Any area of the business that customers see should provide confidence that the service will match up to the same standard. Reception areas should provide refreshments, toilets and waiting areas that are comfortable. Additional facilities could be magazines, WiFi access, toys for children, plasma screens with messages, and advertising materials.
- **Business ambience:** This can also be the corporate image of the business; for example, logos, signs and other distinguishing features, such as specific colours, artefacts, displays and advertising materials. The ambience of the building is also very important. A business offering medical services would have a crisp, clean ambience that demonstrated hygiene, whereas a business offering entertainment should have a relaxed ambience with music playing and bright cheerful colours.

- **Employees:** They should portray the overall image of the business. This could be a uniform; for example, banks, travel agents and supermarkets usually have an employee uniform. Employees should have name badges and always use customers' names when talking to them personally.
- **Customer service:** There should be evidence of customer satisfaction; for example, testimonials, feedback forms, photographs, etc. There should be a written policy of customer service as well as complaints procedures. Contact details as well as telephone numbers should be visible and easily accessible for customers.

- **Company website:** The company mission statement, vision and values should be clearly displayed as well as an organisation chart that shows employees, managers and contact details within the business. Details of awards or quality improvements should be visible to customers to give them confidence. Many of these features can also be displayed on business websites. The website should be well laid out and designed for ease of use.

Quick Fire Questions

1. What are the three additional Ps of the extended marketing mix?
2. What role do employees play in the 'people' part of the extended marketing mix?
3. What physical features should customers experience in the 'physical evidence' part of the extended marketing mix?

Technology in marketing

EPOS for market research

EPOS (electronic point of sale) information can be used extensively for market research. Each bar code scanned gives detailed information on the product being sold, where it is being sold and when. If this information is combined with a loyalty card then even more information can be gathered; for example, the date of birth of the person buying the item. This builds a huge database of information for marketing purposes about what is popular and selling well. However, taking time to gather and process the information costs money and the information can become very quickly out of date in a fast-moving business environment.

Online survey

Electronic surveys are growing in popularity. More and more businesses and organisations are gathering market research information online. Electronic surveys can be carried out in the following ways:

- sending emails to customers asking for replies to certain questions
- feedback forms on websites
- sending SMS messages, asking for customers to provide ratings
- using survey websites such as Survey Monkey.

Internet advertising

Businesses can advertise via their own websites, but also through hyperlinks from other websites and through search engines. The main advantages of advertising on the internet are outlined below:

- a global audience can be reached very quickly
- online advertisements are sophisticated with sound and graphics
- customers can be reached in many ways; for example, through tablets, smartphones, iPads
- social networking sites give advertisers opportunities to target specific groups
- customers can be targeted for recommended purchases depending on what they have bought in the past.

TOP TIP

Targeted online advertising is extremely effective as it allows the customer to interact with the advertiser in their own homes, often just a click away from a purchase.

E-commerce

E-commerce is the term given to buying and selling on the internet, mainly through websites and apps. Businesses advertise their products and services for sale and provide the customer with the facility for ordering and paying for the goods electronically. This is a major area of growth. The advantages are that customers can order where and when they want and have their goods delivered to their home or place of work or to an agreed place (for example, Amazon parcels). Businesses can save on their costs and overheads by reducing the number of high street stores they have to finance. The costs are that deliveries can get lost or stolen and that additional costs are payable for vans and lorries to transport the goods.

Email and databases

Email can be used extensively in marketing in order to keep in contact with customers. Businesses hold databases of customers that can then be used to send targeted and direct mail with information about the business' goods and services. Customers can be emailed with details of new products and services and they can be offered free samples, free gifts and entry into competitions. The advantages of email are that it is quick and easy to email customers using mail merge and large numbers of customers can be reached. The costs are that not everyone reads or responds to emails, especially if they end up in junk email folders.

Social media

The use of social media for advertising and marketing has increased in popularity. Businesses can stay in regular contact with customers on a daily basis in order to provide them with information about products and services and to get feedback from their customers. Popular social media sites include Facebook, Twitter and Instagram. The benefits are immediate contact with customers for relatively low costs. The drawbacks are that social media campaigns can quickly become negative and attract a poor reputation for the business, which takes a lot of effort to try and reinstate.

Desktop publishing (DTP)

The use of DTP to prepare marketing information is easy and straightforward. Even the smallest of businesses can use leaflets, flyers, business cards and brochures to make their business stationery attractive and professional. This can be easily emailed to customers to make them aware of the products and services of the business. This is an easy and relatively cheap way to promote the business.

Text alerts

Customers can choose to have alerts sent to them by text for a variety of reasons. They can be to notify the customer that an item has come back into stock, or that an order has been received or dispatched. They can also be used by banks and building societies for movement on accounts. Customers can sign up for text alerts to keep them up to date. The main advantage is ease of communication for both the customer and the business but the drawbacks are that many customers ignore them or that mobile phone numbers are out of date.

Apps

More and more businesses are creating apps for mobile phones and tablets. Apps are easy to access and use and allow customers to order and pay for goods and services as well as tracking the progress of their order. The main advantages are ease of use and flexibility. Apps can be quickly updated and upgraded without major inconvenience. However, it costs the business time and money to keep investing in the development of the apps.

QR codes

Quick response (QR) codes enable customers to access business links quickly and easily. They can be used by smartphones to read the information and the main advantage is their versatility in providing information. The main costs are that you must have a smartphone and access to the internet in order to be able to read the QR code.

Quick Fire Questions

1. Outline two ways of carrying out an electronic survey.
2. Outline two drawbacks of an electronic survey.
3. Describe e-commerce.

Sample Examination Question

It is becoming more popular to purchase products online. Explain the advantages to an organisation of selling products over the internet.

4 marks

Inventory management

The purpose of an inventory management control system is to ensure that all stocks of raw materials are ordered on time and are kept in excellent condition until they are needed in the production process. This is necessary to ensure that the business does not lose money in unwanted or wasted raw materials or stock items. It is also necessary to keep stock safe from theft. The main features of an inventory control system are that stock levels are set as below:

Maximum inventory level	This is the highest level of stock that the business will hold, in order to minimise costs and make the most efficient use of the space. The level depends on usage and delivery times.
Minimum inventory level	This is the lowest level that stock should not fall below, in order to make sure that there are no shortages, and production does not have to be stopped. The level depends on usage.
Re-order level	This is the level at which more stock should be ordered, in order to make sure that stock does not drop below the minimum level.
Re-order quantity	This is the amount of stock that is ordered, in order to bring the stock back up to the maximum level.
Buffer inventory	This is usually set above the minimum inventory level and allows some stock to be available in case there are problems with deliveries. Buffer inventory means that production does not have to stop.
Lead time	This is the amount of time it takes between ordering new stock and the stock arriving in the business.

Just-in-time (JIT) inventory control

TOP TIP

JIT stock control is sometimes referred to as JIT production.

The features of a just-in-time inventory control system are as follows:

- Stocks are not held in warehouses.
- Stocks are ordered on a regular basis to arrive when they are needed (just-in-time).
- There are regular deliveries – often on a daily basis.
- Suppliers need to be highly reliable.

The benefits and costs of this system are shown in the table below:

Benefits	Costs
JIT avoids warehouse costs or stock room costs, and therefore production costs are lower.	Suppliers must be reliable for stocks to arrive on time.
JIT avoids deterioration of stock that has not been stored properly.	It can be difficult to respond quickly to changes in demand.
JIT avoids stocks going out of date or fashion too quickly.	Administration and ordering systems must be reliable.
JIT avoids theft or pilfering of stock, therefore improving profit figures.	Delays in transport or adverse weather conditions can hold up deliveries.

Storage and warehousing of inventory

Stock warehouses and storage areas need to have the right conditions so that stocks are not damaged.

Stock storage conditions are outlined below.

- The warehouse or stock room should be well lit, dry and well ventilated.
- A system should be used for booking stock in and out of the warehouse.
- Stock should be used on a first in, first out basis.
- Accurate records should be kept of stock levels.
- Warehouses or stock rooms should be supervised and locked.
- Appropriate space should be given to stock items.
- All shelves and storage areas should be labelled for easy access.

Centralised and de-centralised storage and warehousing

Stocks can be held in one central area of the business or spread across different departments or sections.

Centralised inventory storage means that all the inventory is held in one area and expert staff are employed to manage the inventory system. This enhances inventory security and storage. This makes is easier to standardise inventory procedures across the whole organisation and there is more accountability for all stock items. Stock can be bought in bulk from suppliers and favourable discounts obtained for this. However, if the business is very large or spread out it can take time for employees to get to the central area and this can waste time.

De-centralised inventory storage means that all the inventory is held across departments or sections or divisions and each one can adapt their systems to suit their particular needs. This can increase efficiency. However, they may not be able to buy in bulk and receive discounts and it can lead to inconsistencies across the whole of the business.

Logistical management of stock

The process of stock management and control is highly sophisticated and controlled, and is often referred to as **logistics**. This starts at the supply chain and moves through to the consumer receiving the finished product. At each stage in this process, costs and profits are essential – therefore waste has to be avoided.

The benefits to a business overall of managing stock systems are enormous.

- Customers should always receive their orders on time.
- Stocks of raw materials should never run out.
- Administration costs should be controlled, as stock is ordered at regular intervals.
- There is less possibility of under- or over-stocking.
- Less storage space is needed for stock, therefore costs can be reduced.
- There will also be less wastage and theft of stock.

Quick Fire Questions

1. What is meant by JIT stock inventory?

2. Outline two costs and two benefits of JIT stock inventory.

3. Explain the role of suppliers in a JIT inventory control system.

4. Explain the terms maximum and minimum stock.

5. Describe the features of a suitable inventory warehouse.

Sample Examination Questions

1. Explain the problems that can arise from 'under' and 'over' stocking. **4 marks**

2. Discuss the use of just-in-time production. **6 marks**

Methods of production

Production of finished goods can be either labour intensive or capital intensive.

- In **labour intensive** production, people do most of the production, rather than machines. People use their skills and knowledge, although there may be some use of machinery.
- In **capital intensive** production, machines are mostly used – normally in factories with production lines and very large numbers of products produced.

TOP TIP

Be clear about the difference between labour intensive and capital intensive production.

Capital intensive production can be **mechanised** (using machines, but with people involved) or **automated** (systems where there are no humans involved in the production process at all and robots and machinery do all the work).

Type of production	Benefits	Costs
Labour intensive	• Humans can use their skills and abilities and their initiative. • Humans are able to respond to changes quickly.	• Humans are expensive to pay and train. • Absenteeism can cost the business. • Humans can make errors and need rest breaks.
Capital intensive	• Machines can work 24 hours a day. • Machines can do boring repetitive jobs with a high degree of accuracy.	• Machines are expensive to install and maintain. • When machines break down, production stops. • It is difficult to adapt machines quickly to changes in the product.

Methods of production

Production can be organised in three different ways: job production, batch production and flow production. The three methods and the reasons for using them are outlined below.

Job production

This is usually defined as one 'job' done at a time by an individual skilled worker. The job is often made to the specific requirements of the customer, which are agreed in advance. The job involves a high degree of skill on behalf of the employees and the job can take a long time to complete.

Advantages	Disadvantages
The product is made to the specific requirements of the customer.	Can take a long time to produce.
High prices can be charged for the skill and expertise involved.	Production costs are also high because there are no opportunities for economies of scale to be made.

Batch production

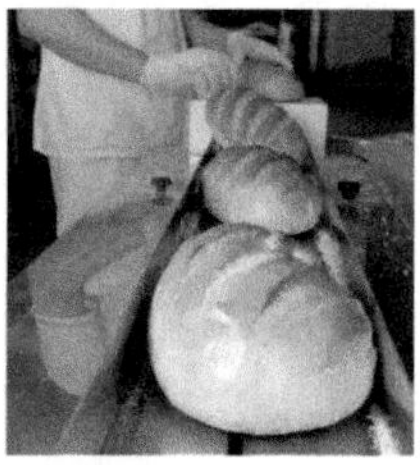

This is usually defined as groups of products that are made at the same time – in batches. Each product in the batch is the same, but there may be slight variations between batches. Batch production is commonly used in the food industry, but also for other products such as paint and wallpaper.

Advantages	Disadvantages
Production costs can be reduced because many products can be made at the same time.	Switching between batches can be time-consuming if changes to machinery need to be made.
There can still be some degree of tailoring the batches to the customer's requirements.	If there is a problem with one product in the batch, the whole batch may be affected.

Flow production

This is usually defined as very large numbers of products produced continuously on a production line. It is often referred to as 'mass production' or 'line production', as the goods are made on production lines. Flow production is common in the car industry, where cars are made in stages along the production line with the use of robots and machinery.

Advantages	Disadvantages
Very large numbers of products can be made quickly at the same time, thus lowering unit costs of production.	The product is exactly the same for each customer – there is no tailoring to their requirements.
The use of machinery allows the production process to be running constantly (often fully automated).	There are very few opportunities for employees to use their skills and initiative – many of the tasks involved are boring and repetitive.
Quality assurance can be built into each stage of the production process.	There are very high costs involved for machinery and production lines.

Quick Fire Questions

1. Distinguish between labour intensive and capital intensive production.
2. Distinguish between mechanisation and automation.
3. Give examples of job, batch and flow production.
4. Outline one advantage and one disadvantage of batch production.
5. Outline one advantage and one disadvantage of flow production.

Sample Examination Questions

1. Describe three different types of production that could be used by an organisation. **3 marks**
2. Explain the advantages and disadvantages of using job production. **3 marks**

Quality

Quality means different things to different people. A quality product involves the following:

- using high quality raw materials
- training employees regularly and to a high standard
- using up-to-date machinery and equipment
- appropriate packaging
- the product being delivered on time
- being produced to quality standards, such as the BSI Kitemark.

Quality circles

This involves groups of employees coming together with the management in order to discuss issues of quality. Employees are usually trained to identify, analyse and solve some of the problems in their work. They would then present solutions to management and, where possible, implement the solutions themselves. One of the aims is to give employees more responsibility and increased motivation.

Quality control

This involves checking products after they have been produced to make sure they meet the standards expected. If a product fails the quality check, it is discarded or recycled back into the production process. Quality control can be wasteful if it is only carried out at the end of the production process.

Quality assurance

This involves a planned and systematic approach to checking products at more regular intervals during the production process and trying to avoid problems happening in the first place. Quality assurance involves the whole production process, starting with good quality raw materials. If quality assurance checks are carried out, employees are more confident that the completed product will be acceptable to customers.

Quality management (continuous improvement)

This involves every employee in the organisation ensuring that quality is built in at each and every stage of the production process. It is an overall business philosophy designed to ensure customer satisfaction. It ensures that quality raw materials are purchased from reliable suppliers. Any errors or problems in the production process are eliminated and the failure rate of finished products is very low indeed.

All staff, including office staff, are involved in the quality process. Often, organisations have quality awards for their high standards, such as: Investors in People, Charter Marks or the BSI Kitemark. Customers know, therefore, that the product is good quality.

TOP TIP

Make sure you understand the difference between quality control, quality assurance and quality management.

Quality standards and symbols

In the UK there are recognised systems of quality standards; for example, the BSI (British Standards Institution) Kitemark scheme. British Standards cover a wide range of businesses and products. These are displayed as logos on products to give an assurance of quality. There are other trade logos that can be displayed, for example, on food products such as beef and eggs, on buildings and electronic products.

Benchmarking

Benchmarking is an approach to quality that involves the business applying a set of standards or benchmarks. The business has to make sure that it achieves these benchmarks in order to stay competitive. Benchmarking can be internal or external.

Internal benchmarking involves setting standards within the organisation that are then used to compare performance across different departments. External benchmarking involves setting standards within the industry for each business to measure themselves against.

Mystery shopping

The use of a mystery shopper has grown in recent years as an indicator of quality. This can be used to gauge the quality of a product or a service. Typically, a member of the public is trained to act as a 'normal' shopper, when in fact they are analysing and evaluating their shopping experience or the quality of the product. The employees of the business are unaware that this is taking place, so very important and accurate feedback can be received about the customer experience.

Costs and benefits of ensuring quality

Benefits	Costs
• Customers will be more satisfied, therefore they will be willing to return and to pass on the good reputation of the business. • Employees will be more satisfied and more motivated in their jobs. • Good quality products will reduce waste. • Profits can be increased.	• Higher costs of raw materials. • Staff training costs. • Costs of applying and maintaining quality awards and standards. • Employees can be reluctant to constantly strive for improvements if they feel under pressure.

Quick Fire Questions

1. Outline the meaning of the term quality.
2. Describe the following – quality control, quality circles.
3. How does quality management ensure customer satisfaction?
4. Describe how benchmarking works.
5. What are the advantages of using a mystery shopper?

Sample Examination Question

Describe quality management systems that can be used within an organisation.

7 marks

Fairtrade

Businesses are encouraged to adopt fair trade principles and customers often support products that have been produced by fair trade companies or countries. In the UK, the Fairtrade Foundation says:

> **Fairtrade is about better prices, decent working conditions, local sustainability, and fair terms of trade for farmers and workers in the developing world.**
>
> **Our vision is of a world in which justice and sustainable development are at the heart of trade structures and practices so that everyone, through their work, can maintain a decent and dignified livelihood and develop their full potential.**

www.fairtrade.org.uk

Fairtrade products include a range of food products; for example, bananas, coffee, tea, as well as flowers, cotton, etc. The Fairtrade foundation licences products as being fair trade and allows them to display the logo.

Benefits and costs of Fairtrade

Advantages	Disadvantages
Customers are happy to buy fair trade products so there will be increased customer loyalty.	Prices are higher both for the manufacturer who buys fair trade raw materials and the consumer who buys the final product.
Most businesses who are licensed for fair trade enjoy a good reputation and public image, and therefore employees are easier to recruit.	Many of the products have to be transported a long way across the world leading to issues of environmental pollution.

Ethical issues

In addition to fair trade, there are other operational issues that businesses should avoid to be considered ethical. Ethical behaviour is any behaviour that is fair and just and does not have an adverse impact on people or countries. It is also behaviour that does not break the law. Some examples of that are ethical and therefore positive business practices are:

- not using child labour or 'sweat shops' to produce goods
- making sure that all employees are treated fairly and justly; for example, complying with the Equality Act 2010
- making sure that all Health and Safety laws and practices are taken into account, and not cutting corners in order to save money.

Costs of ethical operations	Benefits of ethical operations
• Higher prices to be charged to customers • Higher prices for raw materials	• Customers will be happy to buy from the business so sales and profits may increase • Increased customer loyalty • Motivated employees who will stay loyal to the business

TOP TIP

See page 103 for a full description of the Equality Act 2010.

Quick Fire Questions

1. What is meant by fair trade?
2. How does Fairtrade benefit a business?
3. What is ethical business behaviour?
4. Outline two costs of ethical operations.
5. Outline two benefits of ethical operations.

Ethical and environmental issues

Caring for the environment is now a huge issue for all businesses, covering such areas as pollution, recycling, waste reduction, omission of greenhouse gases and sustainable development. There are laws in place to cover some of these issues, but businesses have to respond to customers' wishes that the environment is not damaged in the production of goods and services.

Environmental issues that businesses **must avoid:**

- **pollution:** smoke, fumes, gases, emissions into the air

- **dumping of waste:** waste must be recycled and disposed of carefully and lawfully
- **using up limited resources:** where possible, sustainable resources should be used.

Business can take the following positive actions.

Recycling

- Recycling allows waste materials to be reused into new products. This means that the world's natural resources have a chance to recover and be renewed.
- Recycled materials can help to save energy in the production process, as products do not require new raw materials.
- Recycling helps to protect the environment, as greenhouse gas emissions can be reduced and there is less need to keep mining and quarrying for new raw materials.
- Recycling also helps to reduce landfill sites. If waste materials are recycled, there is no need to dump them into landfill sites that produce greenhouse gases into the environment.

Reducing packaging

Packaging is really important for the final product in any industry. Packaging helps to protect the product during transportation and also to help protect it while on the shelves. Packaging also helps to sell the product if it is a luxury item, like perfume and makeup. However, reducing unnecessary packaging will cut down on waste and therefore the need for more recycling.

Reducing energy

Reducing running costs and energy will also help the environment, as well as business profits. Cutting out additional lighting and heating, reducing vehicle journeys, and avoiding duplication of processes will go a long way towards reducing the damaging effects on the environment.

<table>
<tr><th>Benefits of environmental responsibility</th><th>Costs of environmental responsibility</th></tr>
<tr><td>Business will gain a good image and positive reputation, which will attract customers and therefore increase sales and profits.

</td><td>Costs of recycling and avoiding dumping of waste.
</td></tr>
<tr><td>Employees will be more satisfied and motivated if they believe the business is operating in the right way.
</td><td>Training and re-training staff to follow ethical and environmental practices.

</td></tr>
</table>

Quick Fire Questions

1. Outline two actions that businesses should avoid in order to help the environment.
2. How does recycling help the environment?
3. Explain how reducing packaging and energy helps businesses and the environment.

Technology in operations

Computer-aided design (CAD)

Computer-aided design (CAD) is the name given to software programs that allow the user to create drawings, plans and blueprints using computers. Architects, graphic designers, engineers and designers can produce drawings of potential projects, such as kitchens, bathrooms, houses, bridges, etc. The software allows zooming in and out and viewing the drawings at different angles. Also, if a change is made to a particular aspect of the drawing, all other aspects can be automatically updated. CAD software can now run on PCs and desktop computers. Professional results can be obtained very quickly.

Computer-aided manufacture

Computer-aided manufacture (CAM) is the name given to manufacturing systems that are automated. The production processes are controlled by a computer that can give precise instructions to machines and robots in the production process. CAM is used extensively in the electronics industry. It is hugely beneficial to the business because of the speed, accuracy and continuity of the machinery and equipment. The use of CAM has often led to a reduction in the number of employees required in a business.

Electronic point of sale (EPOS)

EPOS is short for electronic point of sale. This is the system that is used in major retailers at the point where customers pay for their goods. It is often called an 'electronic checkout'. The EPOS system scans the barcodes on the products, which looks up the price of the item and deducts the item from the total stock balance. A receipt is given to the customer, with all the details of the purchase listed along with other information such as special offers, discount vouchers, etc.

TOP TIP

The use of technology in retailing has changed the way in which businesses interact with their customers. The amount of information available is vast, and consumer behaviour is closely monitored.

For inventory control purposes, EPOS makes stock recording and stock movements very easy. Each item that is scanned at the point of sale is automatically deducted from the total in stock. The computer can generate stock reports to show which items are nearing their re-order level, and which items have sold the most, or the quickest. All the information is available from the database that is 'behind' the stock system. EPOS can also be used by customers accessing the business' website to see if certain items are in stock (for example, Argos or Ikea). Goods can then be held for customers to uplift from the store or they can be delivered to their homes.

Robotics

The use of robots in production is widespread across the world. Robots can be used to perform repetitive and dangerous tasks with precision and accuracy. They can also be used to perform highly complex and skilled tasks; for example, electronics and car manufacturing. The main benefits of robots are the speed and accuracy with which they work and they fact that they can work 24/7 as they do not need to rest or sleep. The main costs of robots are the huge sums of money needed to invest in the technology and the upkeep that is required on a regular basis.

Barcodes and QR codes

The operations function relies heavily on the use of raw materials, parts and components. These can be hugely complex to identify with part numbers, stock codes, etc. Barcodes and QR (quick response) codes can make this process much more straightforward. The main benefits are that inventory management is easier with barcodes and QR codes being scanned and the information processed quickly and easily. The main costs are the technology required to keep this going but also the loss of expertise if employees have to rely on codes rather than knowledge of the individual parts or raw materials being used.

Email, internet and databases

Operations relies on its suppliers for providing quality raw materials at a reasonable price. The operations function will need to email suppliers on a regular basis asking for quotes and information about products and services. Operations will also use the internet to source the best supplier websites and deals on offer. Operations will also use databases to hold details of their suppliers and supplier contacts. The benefits of using these technologies is that the business can stay up-to-date and achieve the best prices. The costs of using these are the time taken to ensure that all the data is up-to-date and stored in line with General Data Protection Regulation (GDPR) regulations.

Quick Fire Questions

1. What is meant by CAD?
2. What are the advantages of using CAM?
3. Explain how EPOS can be used for inventory control.
4. How can customers benefit from EPOS systems at home?

Workforce planning

Elements of workforce planning

- Skills analysis of current staff: the business needs to know the current skills and experience of their existing staff. They should carry out a skills analysis regularly through assessment of the workforce or through appraisals. They also need to know if any staff are due to retire or leave the business and whether they need to be replaced.
- Staffing forecast to meet demand: the business needs to know the current and future demand for their products and services so that they can plan to have the staff skilled and trained. Are there products and services being introduced into the market that require new training for staff? Are they discontinuing any products or services, meaning that staff have to be retrained in something new? The business should also analyse the labour market to see what is available in terms of specialist staff. For example, sometimes it can be difficult to recruit specialist engineers and software developers. The business might have links with universities and colleges to source new employees with the skills required.
- Planning internal and external supply of staff: once the business knows the current demand for its products and services and the level of skills and experience of its current staff, they can start to plan for any new or supply staff they need on a temporary basis.

TOP TIP

Workforce planning is a detailed and comprehensive process, which has to be updated constantly in order to make sure that employees are in the right place, at the right time, with the right skills.

Recruitment

Recruitment is the process of getting potential candidates to apply for a job vacancy.

Recruitment methods

Internal recruitment involves appointing existing employees to new positions within the business – this includes promotion.

External recruitment involves appointing new employees from outwith the business. Jobs are advertised externally and anyone can apply.

Analysis of recruitment methods

	Benefits	Costs
Internal recruitment	• There are no external advertising fees. • Staff are already known to the business. • Less training is required as existing staff already know the organisation.	• Some staff may feel 'passed over' when another member of staff is promoted. • There is no 'fresh blood' brought into the organisation with new ideas. • Higher salaries may have to be paid.
External recruitment	• There is a wider range of applicants with new ideas. • It may be quicker to move the business along in terms of growth and expansion. • If employees have relevant experience, they may not need as much training.	• Costs of advertising externally or using an agency. • Existing staff may feel aggrieved that they have not been considered. • New employees may take a long time to become familiar with the organisation.

Quick Fire Questions

1. Describe the elements of workforce planning.

Selection of employees

The selection process

Once all the applications and CVs have been received from candidates, the selection process begins to find the best person to fill the job vacancy. In the first instance, the applications have to be cross-checked with the person specification to ensure that the candidates meet all the criteria. Those who do not will be discarded at this point. The business then has to decide the best way in which to select the best candidate. There are different methods of selection and there is also the possibility of using an assessment centre.

Selection methods

Interview

Candidates will be invited for an interview and an interview panel will be formed. During the interview, each panel member will assess the candidate's answers to a set list of questions and their overall performance. After interviewing all the candidates, the panel will assess the best performance and fit for the business.

Presentation

Candidates may be asked to give a presentation to the panel. This could involve using a flip chart, or a computer and data projector. The topic for the presentation would usually be given to the candidates in advance.

Role play

Candidates may be asked to take part in a scenario that shows how they react in different situations, such as dealing with a difficult customer. The role play is designed to show the strengths, weaknesses and personality of the candidates.

Group interviews

Candidates may be asked to take part in a group interview. This allows the business to see who emerges as a natural leader, but also to see how candidates interact with one another.

Team-building tasks

Candidates may be asked to work as part of a team to solve a particular problem. They would be expected to work together to come up with an acceptable solution. This tests candidates' team-working skills, such as listening, giving instructions, following instructions and interpersonal skills.

TOP TIP

Remember the difference between recruitment and selection. Recruitment stops at the point where candidates have all applied for the job. Selection begins when they start to narrow down the candidates using selection methods.

Psychometric testing

Psychometric tests fall into two main categories: **personality questionnaires**, which try to measure aspects of your personality, and **aptitude tests**, which try to measure your intellectual and reasoning abilities.

Personality tests ask you about your thoughts, feelings and your behaviour in a variety of situations. The tests can be tailored to suit the business; for example, supermarkets would ask questions about dealing with customers, whereas medical tests would ask about dealing with patients. The results of personality tests enable the business to match up personalities with specific jobs.

Aptitude tests cover a range of areas, such as literacy, numeracy, problem-solving and reasoning. Again, the tests can be tailored to suit the business; for example, an engineering business would be interested in numeracy and problem-solving. The results of the tests are more specific than personality tests, as there are likely to be more questions that have a definite answer. The results of these tests are therefore very important in selecting candidates.

Assessment centres

The use of assessment centres has grown in recent years, with some businesses using them to carry out the last stage of the selection process. Assessment centres should not be confused with recruitment agencies, who can provide all stages in the recruitment and selection process.

The assessment centre can be based in the business itself or in a hotel, university or recruitment agency. It is usually somewhere with plenty of space and a relaxing environment. The activities that candidates will undertake can involve:

- group exercises
- in-tray exercises
- presentations
- case studies
- psychometric testing
- social activities, such as lunch and coffee breaks.

The activities can take place over a morning, a full day or maybe even two days, depending on the level of job. After all the activities have been completed, the business or recruiters have a very comprehensive picture of the skills, abilities and personality of the candidates being assessed. They can therefore make very reliable judgments about the best candidate for the job.

Probationary periods

Once candidates have been appointed, the business may wish to stipulate that their appointment is for a trial period or a **probationary period**. This means that the candidate has to demonstrate an acceptable level of performance during this time before they will be appointed permanently. This allows the business to ensure that, at the end of this period, they have the best candidate for the job with a proven track record.

Quick Fire Questions

1. Outline two methods of selecting candidates.
2. Explain the difference between recruitment and selection.
3. What are the advantages of using team-building and group discussion to select candidates?
4. Outline how a psychometric test measures personality and aptitude.
5. Name three activities that candidates might undertake in an assessment centre.
6. What is a trial or probationary period?

Sample Examination Questions

1. Describe a selection process that an organisation could use to ensure it employs the best workers.
4 marks

2. Describe the benefits to an organisation of using interviews prior to appointing a new employee.
3 marks

3. Justify **three** forms of testing (other than interviews) in the selection process. (A different justification should be used each time.)
3 marks

Training and development

Staff training and development is highly relevant to all staff no matter what stage of their career or their place in the business. All employees have to be highly skilled and trained to ensure that they continue to do their job to the highest possible standard.

Types of training

- **On-the-job training** is carried out in the workplace. It is undertaken by employees to improve their knowledge, skills and performance at work.
- **Off-the-job training** is carried out away from the workplace. It can be undertaken at college, university, training centres or other venues. It may involve additional qualifications. The training is usually delivered by experts in their field.
- **Induction training** is usually carried out in the workplace. It is offered to new employees and can include information about the wider business environment as well as specific training about the new job.

TOP TIP

Be clear about the difference between types and methods of training.

Methods of training

Whichever type of training is undertaken, it can be delivered in a variety of ways.

- **Lectures** are often used with off-the-job training to reach large numbers of people at the same time. They are a useful way of giving information.
- **Role playing and simulation** enable employees to react in a realistic way to solving customer problems or dealing with other colleagues. Employees are asked to 'play out' a scenario in order to learn from this.
- **Job rotation** involves moving an employee through a series of jobs so they can get a good feel for the tasks that are associated with different roles.
- **Apprenticeships** are especially appropriate for jobs requiring production skills; for example, plumbing, engineering, etc. However, they are also used now for young employees in administration and business roles.
- **Multimedia** training can take a variety of different forms, such as DVDs, PowerPoint presentations, films, computer simulations, etc. Many of these can be undertaken by the employee in their own time away from work.

Benefits and costs of training

All forms of training – no matter where or when they take place – contribute to the business or organisation achieving their strategic objectives. Training leads to greater efficiency and effectiveness, which in turn means that the business can be more competitive in the marketplace.

The table below summarises the benefits of training.

Employer	Employee
Higher skilled, more effective employees leads to reductions in customer complaints.	Increased skills and knowledge, therefore greater effectiveness in their job.
Higher skilled, more effective employees leads to reductions in absenteeism and staff turnover.	Increased morale and motivation at work, therefore higher productivity.
Higher skilled, more effective employees will be ambitious and will apply for vacancies, therefore reducing the skills gap.	Increased confidence and possibility of promotion or salary increases based on performance.

The table below summarises the costs of training.

Employer	Employee
Cost of paying for trainers/college/ university.	Time taken away from work, which means they have to catch up when they return.
Cost of paying for employees who are away from work attending the training.	Training might not be exactly what the employee needs and is therefore a waste of time.
Cost of travelling and accommodation expenses paid to employees.	Employee might find it difficult to remember all aspects of training if they are trained away from their place of work.

Graduate and corporate training schemes

Many large businesses run graduate and corporate training schemes in order to develop potential in their employees as future leaders and managers in the organisation.

University graduates can apply for a graduate training scheme that will be tailored to the specific business or industry that the business operates in. The graduate training scheme may lead to additional qualifications. The scheme will enable the employee to develop skills and knowledge that they will use in that particular job.

Corporate training schemes are similar but they are for everyone in the business whether they are a university graduate or not. The business will offer specific training for employees to improve their skills and knowledge and this can lead to future promotions.

CPD and work-based qualifications

Many business sectors allow employees to work and study for qualifications at the same time. There are many examples from professional occupations, such as:

- health
- accountancy
- business
- customer care
- health and safety
- ICT
- horticulture.

Employees are usually taken on with the agreement that they will study for their qualifications at the same time. The level of qualification can vary; for example, apprenticeships are structured training programmes that lead to qualifications relevant to the industry such as plumbing, joinery, etc. Other qualifications can be at degree level; for example, accountancy, ICT. The employee may attend college or university at various times – away from the workplace or in the evenings.

TOP TIP

Make sure if you are asked about the benefits of training that you make it clear whether the benefits are for the employer or the employee.

Types of appraisal

Businesses need to know how their employees are performing in the jobs, so they usually carry out an assessment of their performance. This is known as an appraisal. Employee appraisal takes many different forms and they all have costs and benefits.

Type of appraisal and description	Costs and benefits to employer	Costs and benefits to employee
One to one This is when an employee meets with their line manager for an interview or assessment of their performance.	This takes time away from their job but it means that the employer has a chance to speak openly about their job performance and get to know what is required in terms of training.	The employee might feel nervous about the interview or not get on with the line manager. However, if the interview or assessment is positive, the employee might get a promotion or pay rise.
360 degree This is when an employee asks for extensive feedback from everyone they come into contact with about their job performance. It is often used by managers with their department.	It takes time to gather the information from a variety of sources and some of the information may be anonymous. However, it is extremely useful and can give the employer an in-depth view of their employee's performance.	The employee might feel under enormous pressure to gather information from such a wide variety of sources. However, the feedback can be very uplifting and positive and enable a promotion or pay rise in the future.
Peer to peer This is when employees meet to review and assess each other's performance.	The cost to the employer is that peers might not necessarily be accurate in their assessment of each other, especially if it is negative. The benefits to the employer is that this can work very well if employees feel trusted to carry this out.	The employee might feel that they will not get the best chance of a pay rise or promotion if their peers are carrying out the assessment. However, they might feel more at ease with their peers than with management carrying out the assessment.

Quick Fire Questions

1. Name three types of training.
2. Outline two methods of training.
3. Outline two benefits of training for the employer.

Sample Examination Questions

1. Explain the advantages of staff training for an organisation. **4 marks**
2. Describe the costs of staff training. **4 marks**

Motivation and leadership

Theories of motivation

Employees want to feel motivated at work in order to feel satisfied with their jobs. Employers also want to get the best out of their employees. There are a number of theories that have been put forward over a period of time to outline how this can be achieved.

Motivation theory	Details
Maslow's theory (Abraham Maslow)	Maslow's theory was complex, stating that employees had five levels of human needs to be met at work. These needs were in a hierarchy – the lowest in the hierarchy had to be met first before moving to the next level (see diagram). 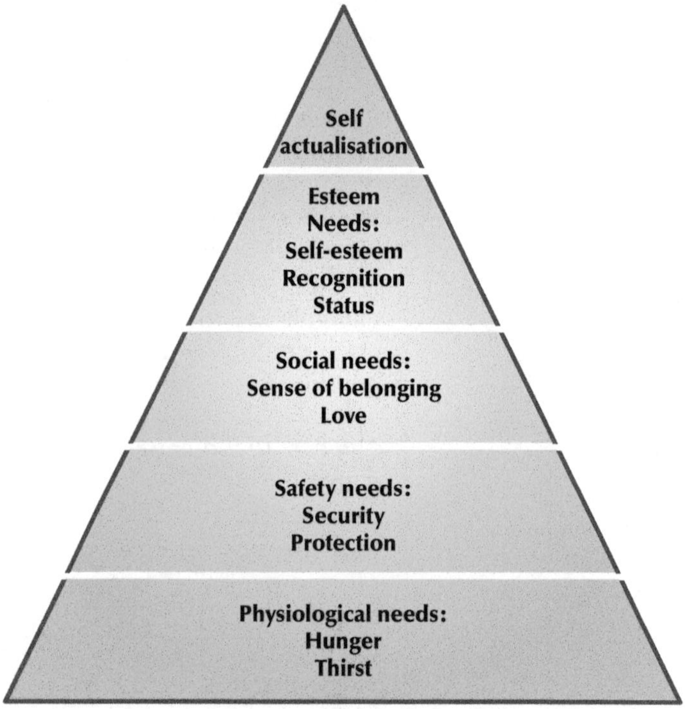
Herzberg's theory (Frederick Herzberg)	Herzberg believed that there were two factors that affect employees in the workplace: i) **motivators**, which motivate employees, such as how interesting the work is; and ii) **hygiene factors**, which do not motivate employees, but would de-motivate them if they were not present, e.g. safe working conditions. Herzberg also believed that the nature of the job should be enhanced by strategies such as job enrichment, job enlargement and empowering employees to feel more responsible.

Motivating staff – role of management

It is important that business owners and managers lead and motivate their staff in order to get the best from them. Motivation comes in a variety of ways – through financial and non-financial rewards, but also through proper leadership and employees feeling a sense of pride and being valued. So, depending on the type of leadership, employees may be motivated or they may lack motivation. Business leaders do not all fit neatly into any one particular category, but a useful analysis of leadership styles is outlined below.

Leadership style	Characteristics
Autocratic	• gives instructions and orders without negotiation or discussion • no real input from employees • employees are not encouraged to use their initiative • can lead to high staff turnover • good system for the army, where orders are given to be followed
Democratic	• managers consult with employees before making decisions • employees feel included and therefore are more motivated • employees can use their initiative • managers may delegate authority to others to make decisions • less staff turnover, as staff are happy at work • can lead to delays in decision making as there are more people involved
Laissez-faire	• managers do not give clear direction to employees as they are 'hands off' and allow employees to make their own decisions • works well if employees are capable of making their own decisions • can be ineffective if employees are inexperienced, and can lead to problems with missing deadlines

Quick Fire Questions

1. Outline two theories of motivating employees.
2. Outline the characteristics of a democratic leader.
3. How do managers help to motivate employees?

Sample Examination Questions

1. Discuss the role of management in motivating staff.

4 marks

Employee relations

Employee relations means encouraging and motivating staff to develop and perform to their potential in their job. It also involves communicating, negotiating and bargaining with staff on a more official basis, through trade unions and works councils. Employee relations can have a positive effect on the success of the business, as staff work well and customers are happy. However, employee relations can also have a negative effect on the success of the business if employees are unhappy and industrial action is being undertaken. Employee relations therefore often involves negotiating with trade unions, when appropriate, to secure positive outcomes.

Positive employee relations

Businesses try to keep their employees motivated in lots of different ways:

- **Works council:** A committee made up of employees and managers, to enable the employees to be consulted and involved in the decision-making process of the business.
- **Team-working:** Employees are given the opportunity to work with others in teams or on specific projects. They share decision making, successes and failures. They learn from each other and build trust and respect.
- **Staff training:** As previously outlined, staff training and development leads to increased efficiency and a higher rate of staff retention.
- **Communication:** Employees value giving their opinions and being listened to. But equally, they do not usually have a difficulty with following instructions provided they are kept informed of decisions and the reasons why they have been made. Many employees say they want transparency in communication.
- **Quality circles:** These groups of volunteer employees discuss how to improve the business. They can be responsible for implementing suggestions on how improvements can be made.
- **Employee of the month and achievement awards:** Many businesses operate schemes whereby employees can receive awards, bonuses or recognition for their role in the business. These can be competition-type events or based on feedback from customers and colleagues.

- **The working environment:** Many businesses have recognised the importance of a positive working environment.
  - They provide areas for relaxation or playing games.
  - Some offer reduced price or free gym membership.
  - Others employ professionals to help with stress management or alternative therapies, such as reflexology.
  - Other arrangements include team-building days out and social events.

TOP TIP

Not every business can offer all of these methods of motivation, but all businesses should try and offer something extra to motivate their employees.

Legal and company policies

Most businesses have policies and processes in place to help employees during times of difficulty. It is important that employees and their representatives are made aware of these policies and how they can impact on employees at work, both positively and negatively.

Grievance and discipline

Employees may experience difficulties at work with their line managers or supervisors or with other colleagues. Usually these difficulties or disputes are settled quickly with talking and negotiation. However, they can escalate and become more formal.

The grievance procedure is in place so that both employers and employees can have their grievance (or complaint) heard in an appropriate manner and that this is settled in the best way possible. This may be carried out by HR officers or by trade unions.

The discipline procedure should be clear and transparent to all employees so that they know what is expected of them in the workplace. If employees break the conditions of their employment, they may be disciplined. This can take the form of a warning, a fine or in very serious cases the employee might be dismissed or even referred to the police.

Absenteeism

Most businesses have support systems in place to provide support to colleagues who need time off work. Employees might be absent for a range of different reasons; for example, stress, bereavement, sickness, illness etc. Absence management procedures usually require the employee to provide adequate explanations for their absence in the form of a doctor's certificate. The employee might need to have a representative with them to help explain the absence. Many businesses conduct 'return to work' interviews to make sure their employees are fit for work and they can be offered a phased return to work if the absence has been a long one. Frequent unexplained absences can lead to the employee being disciplined or ultimately dismissed.

Redundancy

From time to time, businesses may need to make their employees redundant. This could be due to falling sales or closure of the business altogether. Redundancy can be a stressful and frightening experience for employees, who fear they will not get another job. Other employees may see redundancy as a way of starting afresh somewhere else or a new career. The business must have proper systems in place to ensure that all employees are given the correct information and compensation if they are made redundant.

Quick Fire Questions

1. Explain the term employee relations.
2. Outline two support systems that can be put in place for employees.
3. Explain how the working environment can help employees stay motivated.
4. What is the purpose of employee appraisals?
5. What would be the result if a business did not try and motivate their employees?

Sample Examination Questions

1. Appraisal has identified poor performance for a member of staff. Describe the actions that a manager could take to improve the employee's performance.
6 marks

2. Explain the effects that poor employee relations could have on an organisation.
4 marks

Role of trade unions

A trade union is an organisation that employees can join for support, usually to help them negotiate better pay and conditions. A trade union will advise its members, help resolve disputes with employers and offer additional benefits such as financial services and legal advice.

Industrial action

There are different methods of industrial action – some more damaging than others. All forms of industrial action penalise the business, but employees can also suffer through loss of earnings.

- **Strike:** Employees refuse to go to work but do not get paid.
- **Overtime ban:** Employees refuse to work overtime and lose pay.
- **Sit-in:** Employees occupy the premises and normal work cannot take place.
- **Work to rule:** Employees only do exactly what their contract states. Goodwill is damaged and some overtime payments may be lost.
- **Go slow:** Employees still carry out their duties but do so more slowly or with reduced productivity.

TOP TIP

There can be positive benefits from industrial action; for example, introducing new procedures that all employees will follow and be happy with.

Role of ACAS

When industrial disputes cannot be resolved, businesses can ask for direct help from an organisation called ACAS. ACAS provides information, advice, training, conciliation and other services to help prevent or resolve workplace problems.

Their overall aim is to improve employee relations and to help disputes from arising in the first place or escalating after they have begun. Often ACAS provides **arbitration**, where both sides in the dispute ask for an agreement to be reached that they can both adhere to.

Employee participation

Employee participation is an effective way to give leadership and a voice to the employees of a business. The more employees are involved in the decisions, the more they will take ownership of carrying these out and ensuring that the business objectives are met. This will also increase employee morale and wellbeing. Employee participation takes different formats depending on the type and size of business.

Works councils

These are councils that exist to have a dialogue between the management and employees usually working on the 'shop floor' or production environment. The council knows the working conditions and requirements of the job, therefore they are in the best position to advise management on improvements that need to take place. The council involves both management and employees and is not linked to trade unions.

Worker directors

A business may invite an employee to join the board of directors. The employee's role is to represent the ordinary workers in the business and to have their voice heard at the most senior level in the business. This gives employees a voice and an improved feeling of involvement in the running of the business.

Consultative committees

Businesses may set up consultative committees, which they use to consult between management and employees. Employees are consulted before decisions are taken and their views are sought. This is to enable employees to feel part of the decision-making process. It doesn't necessarily mean that all employee views will be taken into account but management must explain the reasons why they are not doing so.

Employee legislation

There are a number of laws that have to be followed by both employers and employees. The laws are designed to make the working environment safe and to ensure that employees are treated fairly in the workplace as well as having a decent wage. The impact on employees is that working conditions are improved and that wages will rise. The impact on employers is often that costs will rise due to higher wages and ensuring that premises are safe to work in, as well as the costs of training all staff in health and safety measures.

Health and Safety at Work Act 1974

This law outlines the responsibilities of both employers and employees in relation to health and safety at work. Employers have a duty to:

- provide and maintain safety equipment and safe systems of work
- ensure materials used are properly stored, handled, used and transported
- provide information, training, instruction and supervision
- provide a safe place of employment, e.g. fire extinguishers, protective clothing
- appoint health and safety representatives.

If employees felt that their employer was not carrying out their duties properly in terms of the law, they can complain to the Health and Safety Executive (HSE) or to their trade union representative. Employees will be at risk if they are not properly trained or do not have proper safety equipment. Employees have a duty to:

- take reasonable care of the health and safety of themselves, and of others who may be affected by what they do/do not do
- co-operate with the employer on health and safety matters.

The Equality Act 2010

The Equality Act 2010 bans unfair treatment and helps achieve equal opportunities in the workplace and in wider society. It brings together previous Acts that deal with discrimination, and makes it unlawful to discriminate against anyone on the grounds of sex, race, marital status, religion and belief, disability, sexual orientation or pregnancy.

A business or organisation has to make sure that when recruiting they do not have any bias or prejudice in their job descriptions or person specifications. They must ensure that candidates are not disadvantaged during recruitment and selection procedures, for example, with limited access for wheelchairs to the building. They must provide all the necessary support for employees to do their job without discrimination.

National Minimum Wage Regulations

This law was passed to ensure that employees receive a minimum wage in order to avoid poverty and exploitation. The minimum wage varies depending on the age of the employee but is for **employees under the age of 25**. The rate is set by the government and increases are applied each year.

National living wage regulations

The national living wage applies to all **employees over the age of 25**. All the same reasons and principles apply as to the national minimum wage but setting a rate for employees over the age of 25 takes into account the maturity of individuals and their different circumstances. The rate is set by the government and increases apply each year.

The impact on employers is that their wage costs will rise and they have to find the extra cash to do this, for example raising prices for customers.

Quick Fire Questions

1. What is the purpose of a trade union?
2. Outline two methods of industrial action.
3. Describe two duties of employers under the Health and Safety at Work Act.
4. What is the purpose of the Equality Act 2010?

Sample Examination Questions

1. Describe the main features of the Equality Act 2010.
   3 marks
2. The introduction of new technology may cause unrest in the workplace. Describe four forms of industrial action.
   4 marks

Technology in human resource management

The table below shows the different ways in which technology can be used to increase efficiency in human resources.

Technology	Use and effectiveness
Database 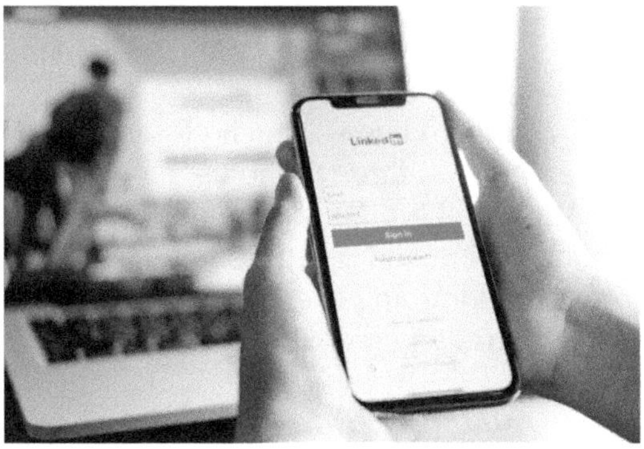	Businesses can store records of all employees with all the necessary details needed. The records can also include training needs, salary details, promotion etc. Records can be searched to find employees who meet certain criteria; for example, those who require training. Records can also be kept of consultants and trainers who regularly interact with the business to provide training. LinkedIn is an online database where individuals post their own details (like a CV or job history). These can be used by businesses to search for suitable candidates for jobs.
Video conferencing 	This can be used in an interview setting to make face-to-face contact with applicants. Interviews can be conducted over long distances without the need to travel. Video conferencing can also be used in training if the trainer is in another location. The training can be delivered to several employees at the same time. Coaching, mentoring and appraisals can also take place via video conferencing links.
Online application forms 	The facility to apply for jobs online has changed the fundamental role of human resources. So much more information can be obtained from candidates so that selection processes can be more accurate. The applicants also benefit as the application can be completed and sent quickly and right up to the last minute to meet deadlines.

Technology	Use and effectiveness
Job Advertising www.s1jobs.com www.indeed.co.uk https://uk.linkedin.com/	Recruitment websites where jobs are advertised regularly have grown rapidly in the last 10 years, whilst the use of newspaper advertising has declined. Online job advertisements are commonplace on both business websites and job recruitment websites. The most obvious advantages are the ability to reach a wide audience across the world and the ease of gathering the applicants' information online.
e-diary 	Human resources can keep a much closer track of all employees through the use of e-diary. Almost all e-diary information can be shared online and meetings, appointments and training events can be scheduled for times when employees are available.
Presentation software Some examples are: • Apple Keynote • Prezi • Google Slides • Slidebean • Glisser	Presentation software has been in use for a long time but is becoming more sophisticated and sleek for business presentations. Presentation software can be used by applicants for jobs but it can also be used in all training and development events when presenting to employees.
Virtual Learning Environments (VLE)	Staff training, development and learning can take place through the medium of a VLE. This is a web-based resource for employees to access at home or in the workplace. It operates like a classroom and the learner can be put in touch with a trainer or supervisor to help them. Notes, resources, videos and assessments are all loaded onto the system and the learner can work through them at their own pace. The VLE can also carry out testing of the employee and remediation as necessary.

Technology	Use and effectiveness
Electronic testing	The use of online web systems has enabled many businesses to carry out testing of their employees or applicants for jobs. The testing can take many different formats; for example, multiple choice, short responses etc. The employer and employee can get instant feedback and the employee's progress can be recorded.

Costs and benefits of using technology

Costs of using technology	Benefits of using technology
Costs of equipment and software	Access to a wider source of applicants worldwide
Costs of maintenance of equipment and software	Access to a wider source of learning materials
Costs of training staff	Increased efficiency in data management
Difficulties experienced if there is a major ICT breakdown	Employees can be more flexible in their work and training

Quick Fire Questions

1. Describe how the following can be used to increase efficiency in human resources:

   Databases

   Video Conferencing

2. Describe the advantages of using online recruitment websites.

Sample Examination Questions

Discuss the advantages and disadvantages of using a VLE to develop the workforce.

4 marks

Sources of finance

Source of finance	Advantages	Disadvantages
Selling of shares This is only available to **limited** companies through selling equity (ownership) on the stock market. The company's memorandum of association and articles of association will set the number of shares that can be issued.	• The shares do not need to be paid back, unlike a loan. • This is an attractive form of investment as it has limited liability.	• Equity or ownership is shared, meaning more people are involved in decision making. • Selling shares makes the organisation vulnerable to a takeover. • Dividends have to be shared amongst a larger group of investors.
Retained profits Once a business has been trading for some time it is likely to have built up reserves of profit that will allow it to reinvest in itself.	• No interest is chargeable. • There is no increase in ownership.	• Money cannot be used for something else. • Stakeholders can be unhappy because they might prefer the funds to be used for them, e.g. dividends for shareholders or increased wages for employees.
Government grants Businesses can qualify for Government/EU grants if they meet certain criteria, e.g. creating employment or becoming more environmentally friendly.	• Grants do not incur interest. • Grants do not have to be paid back.	• Grants are often very difficult and time-consuming to obtain. • Certain criteria need to be met or the grant can be withheld or withdrawn.
Venture capitalist (business angels) Other organisations or wealthy individuals invest in a business for a return on their investment.	• Finance can sometimes be available from venture capitalists when other lenders consider it too risky. • Sometimes the money comes with expertise and advice.	• A return must be made to the investor. • Often there are stipulations with the investment that will limit the freedom of the board of directors.
Leasing or hire purchase Rather than purchase a fixed asset, the business will rent it. With hire purchase, the asset belongs to the business on the final payment.	• There is no initial large investment. • As long as the product is rented, any faults, breakdowns or maintenance will be fixed by the organisation that is renting out the item. • It gives the business time to see if it really needs the asset. • Updated models might become available.	• Costs could be higher in the long-term. • If payments are not maintained, the asset will be repossessed.

Source of finance	Advantages	Disadvantages
Mortgage This is a loan secured on a fixed asset, normally property. 	• This can secure a large amount of funds, which the lender is happier to lend because of the security. • Long period for repayment.	• If payments are not made, then the fixed asset will be sold to recover the debt. • Interest rates are likely to change over time, going up as well as down. • Often larger deposits are required by the borrower to secure the best interest rates.
Bank loan A negotiated loan from a bank paid over a period of time with interest.	• Set payments support effective budgeting.	• Interest is added to the sum borrowed. 
Sale of assets Assets can be sold to release cash	• The cash is available for other things.	• The assets might be needed again in the future.
Bank overdraft This is where more money is removed from the bank than is available. 	• It is often the only form of finance available. • It is often a quick way to obtain funds for a short period of time. • Interest is only charged on the amount outstanding, so early payments will reduce costs.	• There is a higher interest rate than a normal bank loan. • It can reduce the chances of other finance from the bank.
Trade credit In business, it is common practice to purchase items on credit and pay for them later.	• This allows a period where costs are not charged, helping cash flow.	• The business will not be able to take advantage of cash discount, which is a saving for prompt payment. • The amount must still be paid.

Source of finance	Advantages	Disadvantages
Debt factoring Debts are sold to a third party at a discount or subject to an administration fee.	• Funds are available sooner. • Transfers any risk of the debtor defaulting to the third party.	• Less money is received from the debt.
Debentures This is a loan that is given to a business by individuals and is a long-term source of finance.	• The business can use the funding knowing that it has the finance for a long period of time.	• The debenture holder usually has to be paid interest and the debenture usually has to be paid back at some time in the future.
Crowdfunding This is finance that is raised by online appeals. The idea is that lots of people will donate a small amount to the project or cause.	• Large amounts of cash can be raised fairly quickly as many individuals will donate small amounts if they believe in the cause.	• Some crowdfunding projects have equity attached to them, meaning individuals ask for a share in the business before they will invest.

Factors that determine the source of finance

Businesses will select the sources of finance that are most suitable for them and for the type and size of business that they are. The following factors will be taken into account by the business.

- Ease of obtaining the source of finance; for example, a successful business can easily obtain a bank loan.
- The amount of finance the business is looking for. The business might have to consider more than one source of finance.
- The length of time they have to pay back the finance. The business might need a very long-term source of finance, in which case an overdraft is not suitable.
- The amount of interest that they have to pay back. Loans that carry high rates of interest may not be suitable.
- The conditions attached to the source of finance; for example, a government grant might have criteria that the business cannot meet.

Quick Fire Questions

1. Suggest a benefit of selling shares.
2. What is the advantage of a grant over a loan?
3. Can you suggest an advantage over leasing a fixed asset rather than buying it?
4. Describe debt factoring.

Sample Examination Question

Justify three sources of finance.

6 marks

Cash budgeting

A cash budget is a prediction of the flow of cash in and out of an organisation. Budget is normally shown for a quarter of a year (3 months). The purpose of cash budgets is to identify periods when cash flow might be a problem and therefore enable them to take corrective actions, such as applying for a loan or delaying capital expenditure. Cash budgets can also be used to suggest periods where there will be spare funds that can be put to some positive use.

As the name suggests, cash budgets look at cash coming in and going out of the organisation. Most businesses will conduct transactions on credit – delaying payment until some future date. Credit payments will only be recorded in a cash budget at the point it is predicted that cash will actually be received.

Positive cash flow is absolutely crucial to the success of a business. Failure to have enough cash to meet the demands of creditors (those to whom the business owes money) will result in business being forced into liquidation. The cash budget helps decisions to be made.

Below is an example of a cash budget.

This is the cash at the start of the month.

List of actual cash received.

Opening balance plus all cash in.

Cash paid out

This is the total cash at the end of the month. Total cash flow less total cash out.

	£ Month 1 (£)	£ Month 2 (£)	£ Month 3 (£)
Opening balance	**4,000**	**4,000**	**(2,500)**
<u>Cash in</u>			
Sales cash	3,500	2,000	1,000
Sales credit	2,500	3,000	1,000
Loan			10,000
Total cash in	6,000	5,000	12,000
Total cash in	**10,000**	**9,000**	**9,500**
<u>Cash out</u>			
Purchases cash	1,200	1,200	1,200
Purchases credit	1,300	1,300	1,300
Wages	2,000	2,500	3,000
Rent	1,000	1,000	1,000
Utility bills	500	500	500
Purchase of new machinery		5,000	
Total cash out	**6,000**	**11,500**	**7,000**
Closing balance	**4,000**	**(2,500)**	**2,500**

The closing balance for one month becomes the opening balance of the next.

TOP TIP

- 'Balance' means total.
- Brackets tend to show a negative figure.

A positive closing balance is known as a **surplus** and a negative closing balance is a **deficit**.

At Higher you will need to be able to interpret and offer solutions to potential cash flow problems.

The table below explores the possible problems and solutions to the cash budget shown on page 111.

Problem	Possible solutions
Sales are falling while purchases are constant	• Reduce purchases (raw materials) to reflect falling sales. • Find a cheaper supplier of raw materials. • Encourage debtors, those who have bought sales on credit, to pay quicker by offering cash discounts. • Take advantage of the full credit period to delay paying for purchases. • Encourage sales by advertising.
Deficit cash balance in month 2	• Arrange the loan a month earlier. • Rent or lease new machinery rather than buy it.
Rising wage bill at the time of falling sales	• Reduce working hours. • Ban overtime payments. • Change payment system to be based on sales. • Terminate employment contracts, e.g. temporary staff. • Move production to another country with cheaper costs.
Month 2 – purchase of new machinery at a cost of £5,000	• The new machinery could be purchased over a period of time, therefore spreading the cost, or the business could think about leasing the machinery instead to spread the cost.

Quick Fire Questions

1. Explain why a cash budget is used.
2. What is the difference between a 'surplus' and a 'deficit' in a cash budget?
3. Suggest one way of solving a negative cash flow in a business.
4. Give examples of expenses in running a business.

Sample Examination Questions

1. Describe reasons for cash flow problems that can affect an organisation.
5 marks
2. Describe the actions that could be taken to overcome cash flow problems.
5 marks
3. Describe reasons why an organisation would use cash budgets.
5 marks

Financial statements

Two of the most important financial statements that a business has to prepare are **the Income Statement** and **Statement of Financial Position**.

The **Statement of Financial Position** shows the overall value of the business in terms of net worth.

Income Statement

The **purpose** of an Income Statement is to calculate the overall Gross Profit and Profit for the Year (Net Income). The statement is laid out as shown below –

Income Statement for Any Sole Trader for the year ended 31 December	£	£
Sales		525,000
Opening Inventory	45,500	
Add Purchases	315,500	
	361,000	
Less Closing Inventory	75,000	
Cost of sales		286,000
Gross profit		**£239,000**
Expenses		
Staff costs	100,000	
Rent, rates and insurance	75,000	
Heat and lighting	2,500	
Vehicles	12,000	
Total expenses		189,500
Profit for the Year		**£49,500**

The **main elements** of the Income Statement are the calculation of Gross Profit and the calculation of Profit for the Year.

Gross Profit

This shows the profit made after buying in goods and selling them again. This is the profit from trading.

Profit for the Year

This shows the profit made after all the expenses of the business have been deducted.

Gross Profit = Sales – Cost of Sales

Profit for the Year = Gross Profit – Expenses

Statement of Financial Position

The purpose of a Statement of Financial Position is to show the Assets, Liabilities and overall Net Worth of the business. The Statement of Financial Position has several different elements as shown below.

Statement of Financial Position for any Sole Trader as at 31 December		
	£	£
Non-current assets		
Vehicles		28,000
Fixtures and fittings		20,000
		48,000
Current assets		
Inventory	75,000	
Trade receivables	15,500	
Bank	11,000	
Cash	850	
	102,350	
Current liabilities		
Trade payables	12,850	
Working equity (Current assets – Current liabilities)		89,500
Net assets		**£137,500**
Equity		
Opening capital		150,000
Add profit for year		49,500
		199,500
Less drawings		62,000
Closing Balance		**£137,500**

Non-current assets

These are expected to last for a long time such as buildings equipment and vehicles

Current assets

These are cash or near cash items which are used up during the year

Current liabilities

These are debts which the business has to pay back within a short period of time

Working equity/net assets

This is the cash the business has available after the liabilities have been paid

Net Assets is the overall value of the business

Equity

This element shows the overall value of the business to the owner

Interpretation of financial statements

Financial statements are prepared so that the business owners can ask themselves questions about their performance during the year and to decide what course of action they need to take for next year.

Interpretation of an income statement

Questions to be asked may include:

- Is the Sales figure acceptable – are sales too low and if so why?
- Is the Cost of Sales too high – can this be reduced?
- Is the Gross Profit figure acceptable – is it too low and if so why?
- Are Expenses figures too high – can any of them be reduced?
- Is the Profit for Year acceptable?

Interpretation of a statement of financial position

Questions to be asked may include:

- Are there enough assets in the business? Do we need to buy more?
- What are the Trade receivables doing? Are they paying us back quickly enough?
- Do we have enough cash in the bank?
- Do we have too many Trade payables – can we pay back our debts?
- Is the drawings figure too high?
- Is the overall value of the business acceptable given the risks involved?

Users of financial information

There are several different groups of people who can make use of a company's financial information as detailed in the table below:

Stakeholder	Interest in financial information
Employees	• They need to see if their employer is paying a fair wage. • They need to see if the business can afford better working conditions. • They need to judge the security of their job. 
Government agencies	• They need to ensure that correct rates of tax are being paid (HMRC). Multinational companies might try to avoid paying tax in one country where corporation tax is high and declare profits in a country where the tax rate is lower. Governments will need to ensure that this is legal.  • They need to prevent companies taking advantage of a monopoly position, lack of competition, or behaving in an unreasonable way (Competition Commission). • In the case of multinational companies, they need to ensure that businesses are not making unreasonable profits by exploiting their workforce or the environment in less-developed countries. • They need to see if the government can help businesses that are genuinely in need of financial support or tax breaks. • They need to check that third sector organisations are not abusing their position and are really supporting the causes they have set out to help. • They need to see if they provide value for (tax-payers') money in public sector organisations and identify areas for savings.

Stakeholder	Interest in financial information
Owners/ shareholders	• They need to make sure there is a fair return on their investment. • They need to judge how successful the management are. • They need to decide if they should continue to invest. 
Lenders	• They need to judge if the business can pay back borrowed money.
Suppliers	• They need to decide on the degree of credit to give. (*Credit terms are the period of time before a customer needs to pay for goods purchased from them.*)
General public	• They need to see how secure the organisation is and whether it will continue in the future. • They need to check the amount spent on social responsibility.

Quick Fire Questions

1. Name the statements that are referred to as the financial statements.
2. How is gross profit calculated?
3. How is profit for year calculated?
4. Give an example of two common business expenses.

Sample Examination Question

Describe financial information that potential shareholders could use to decide whether or not to invest in a company.

6 marks

Ratio analysis

The purpose of ratios is to compare one figure with another. They are applied when comparisons are being made:

- between similar businesses
- against the industrial average
- within the same business, but between different years.

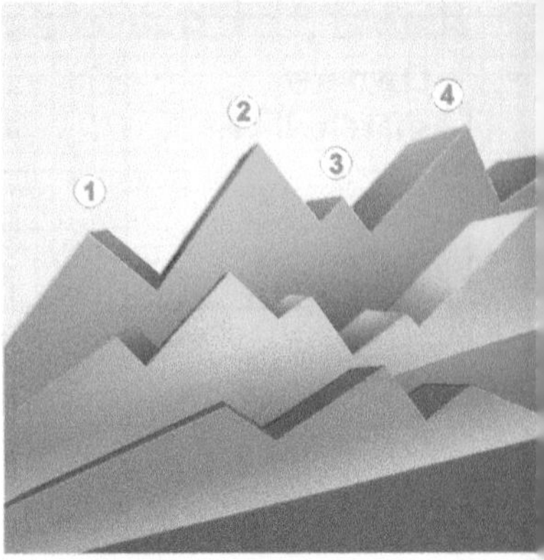

Different ratios can be used to measure different aspects of the business and fall into three general categories.

1. **Profitability ratios:** measuring the value of profit.
2. **Liquidity ratios:** showing the organisation's ability to meet its short-term debts.
3. **Efficiency ratios:** indicating how efficient the business has been in using its resources.

Profitability ratios

Profitability ratios are expressed as a **percentage**. A rising percentage or a bigger percentage than a rival is **good**.

Ratio	Formula	Interpretation	Reasons for improvements
Gross profit percentage	$\frac{\textit{gross profit}}{\textit{sales}} \times 100\%$ This ratio shows the amount of profit the business makes simply from buying and selling.	• A rise in this percentage would be indicating that the business is making more profit in relation to cost of sales. • A decrease would indicate the opposite.	• higher selling price • lower cost of sales because of cheaper suppliers • lower cost of sales through better stock management, e.g. lower stock levels or less waste and/or theft
Profit for year percentage	$\frac{\textit{profit for year}}{\textit{sales}} \times 100\%$ This ratio shows the amount of profit the business earns after paying expenses.	• An increase in this percentage would show more profit in relation to all expenses. • A fall would suggest problems with expenses.	• an increase in the gross profit percentage • a fall in expenses in relation to the amount of sales*

*Sometimes expenses have to rise to increase sales, e.g. paying for more advertising. A positive net profit would indicate that sales have risen more than expenses.

Ratio	Formula	Interpretation	Reasons for improvements
Return on equity employed (percentage)	$\frac{\textit{profit for the year}}{\textit{owners' equity}} \times 100\%$ This ratio shows the maximum percentage return the shareholders could gain from their investment.	• An increase would suggest the business has done well, making a healthy profit. • A fall in the percentage would suggest problems to do with falling sales or rising expenses.	• increase sales revenue without increasing the cost of sales by the same percentage • reducing expenses in relation to sales

Liquidity ratios

Liquidity ratios show the ability of a business to meet short-term debts. They are normally shown as a **ratio**. There are generally recognised ideal ratios, reducing the need for comparisons.

Ratio	Formula	Interpretation	Reasons for improvement
Current ratio	$\frac{\textit{current assets}}{\textit{current liabilities}} : 1$ This ratio shows the ability of the business to pay short-term debts. The ideal ratio is 2:1.	• A figure close to the ideal would suggest the business could meet its immediate debts should it have to. • It might seem strange that a business should not strive to have a much higher number of current assets to current liabilities, but too many current assets would show poor use of these reserves, e.g. large amounts of cash should be invested, 'employed', buying more fixed assets (such as machinery).	• a change in the number of current assets to current liabilities to reflect the ideal ratio of 2:1 • to reduce inventory levels the business could adopt just-in-time (JIT) • be careful not to suggest changes that would have no impact, e.g. encouraging trade receivables to pay would certainly reduce the trade receivables figure, but would simply increase the amount in the bank, resulting in no overall change

Ratio	Formula	Interpretation	Reasons for improvement
Acid test ratio	$\frac{\textit{current assets} - \textit{inventory}}{\textit{current liabilities}} : 1$ This ratio shows the ability of the business to pay short-term debts once inventory is removed. The ideal ratio is 1:1.	• The inventory figure is removed because stock is the most difficult to turn into cash. • A figure close to the ideal would suggest the business is being cautious.	• see current ratio reasons, with the obvious exception of inventory in any analysis

TOP TIP

When carrying out ratio analysis, try to use more than one ratio.

Efficiency ratios

Efficiency ratios are expressed as a **number of times**, with the greater number normally regarded as better.

Ratio	Formula	Interpretation	Reasons for increase
Rate of inventory turnover	$\frac{\textit{cost of sales}}{\textit{average inventory}} = \textit{'times'}$ Average inventory = (closing inventory + opening inventory) ÷ 2 This ratio shows the number of times that the entire inventory is sold out during the year.	• A rising rate of inventory turnover means that the stock is being sold more quickly, which generally would be regarded as a good thing by most businesses. • This figure should however be compared with profitability ratios, to ensure that the stock is not being given away at the expense of profit.	• increase in the cost of goods sold because of a rise in the cost of purchases • change in inventory management resulting in cheaper inventory or less inventory being held, e.g. move to JIT

Limitations of financial analysis

- The figures are based on historic data, and while past performance is a good indicator of future performance, it is only a guide.
- Making comparisons between different organisations can be difficult because there are often many differences, e.g. size.
- External factors (PESTEC) are not taken into account.
- No consideration is taken of the stage in the product life cycle that the product being sold is at.
- Only financial information is considered, and so human resources are not factored in. For example, the recent retirement of an effective Chief Executive Officer (CEO) would be ignored.

Quick Fire Questions

1. The gross profit percentage for a business is 35% while the industrial average is 40%. Is this good or bad? Explain your answer.
2. How could the gross profit percentage be improved?
3. Suggest a reason for an improvement in the profit for the year.

Sample Examination Questions

1. Describe the limitations of ratio analysis.
5 marks

2. Describe three accounting ratios (a different justification must be used each time).
3 marks

Technology in finance

The use of technology has had a major impact on financial transactions and recordings. The ways in which businesses and individuals make payments has changed remarkably in a very short period of time. Online and mobile banking and payment facilities have enabled instant payments to be made across the world.

The finance function in a business will have a variety of technological solutions working to suit different customers and employees. The table below shows some of these uses.

Technology	How it is used
Spreadsheets 	Spreadsheets can be used to record accounting transactions on a regular basis. They have formulas inserted to calculate and this means that 'what if' scenarios can be rehearsed; for example, what if sales increased by 5%? Spreadsheets can be used to prepare Cash Budgets, Income Statements and Statements of Financial Position. Graphs can be prepared from the spreadsheets to be shown to employees, shareholders and other stakeholders.
Internet banking 	The growth and development of internet banking means that money can be moved quickly and easily from one bank account to another with little delay. Websites, mobile apps and online banking all make this easy for customers and businesses.
BACS payments 	BACS is an electronic system used to make payments directly from one bank account to another. The main two types of payment are Direct Debit and Bacs Direct Credit, and the payments can take up to 3 working days to clear. This means that automatic payments can be set up to pay creditors and to pay employees' wages and salaries.
Sage software 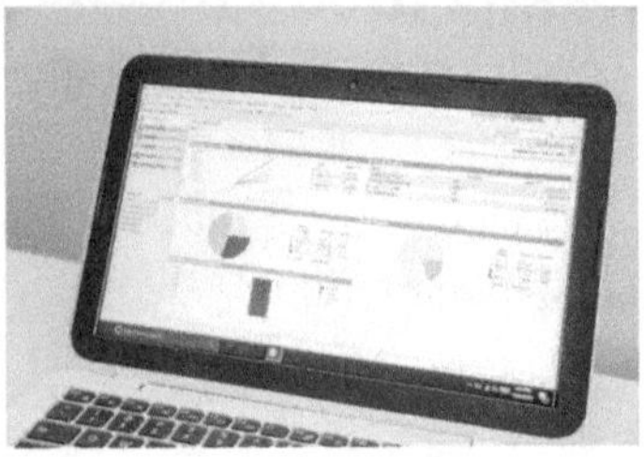	SAGE is a worldwide provider of accounting software and online accounting services for small businesses. The software processes accounting transactions and prepares financial statements and employee wages. It is a comprehensive software accounting solution that makes the finance functions more reliable for a small business.

EFTPOS (electronic funds transfer at point of sale)	The increased use of smartphones had enabled payment technology to advance. EFTPOS transactions are simple and quick in shops, restaurants, bars, petrol stations. Many retailers have updated their technology to allow contactless payments and Apple Pay.

The costs and benefits of technology in finance

The costs are all connected with the actual cash investments that have to be made in the technology – payments for the machinery, software, training and maintenance of the equipment and software. It can also be difficult when systems are down or signals are poor.

The benefits far outweigh the costs in terms of speed and accuracy of processing business payments. Transactions take place instantly across the world and there are audit trails in the form of statements. Cloud facilities for backup also ensure that data is not lost when systems fail or systems are down.

Quick Fire Questions

1. Why would large organisations use spreadsheets?
2. What is the benefit of showing data in a graph?
3. Describe costs associated with technology.

Answers to questions

Page 17 Quick Fire Questions

1 Wealth is created at each stage of the production process by adding value to that stage.

2 Primary sector involves businesses that extract raw materials from the Earth. Secondary sector involves manufacturing raw materials into finished products. Tertiary sector provides services such as health and retail. Quaternary sector involves knowledge-based and scientific services.

3 Public sector is run by government to provide services. Private sector is owned by private individuals to make profit. Third sector is charities and voluntary organisations that do not make a profit.

Page 19 Quick Fire Questions

1 Features of a plc are: owned by shareholders, managed by a board of directors, directors are appointed by shareholders at the AGM, shareholders receive dividends on their shares.

2 Dividends

3 Advantages – shareholders have limited liability, more sources of finance available, economies of scale, increased power in the market. Disadvantages – accounts have to be published, shares can be purchased by anyone, has to abide by Companies Act, significant start-up costs.

4 McDonalds, Pizza Hut, Burger King, Body Shop, Dominos.

5 A multinational company is a business that operates in more than one country.

Page 19 Sample Examination Questions

1 The advantages of operating as a franchise are that the franchisee is able to start a business fairly quickly with an established reputation and customer base. They will benefit from the ideas of other franchisees. They will benefit from economies of scale in terms of cheaper advertising, transport costs.

2 The main characteristics of a multinational corporation are that they operate in more than one country. They usually have headquarters in the 'home country' and operate in 'host countries'. They are very large organisations with a range of staff and expertise. They make use of up-to-date technology and equipment in order to communicate around the world. They offer a wide range of quality products at cheaper prices.

3 Multinationals increase living standards by allowing the host country to access jobs and products and services, however the multinational can be very powerful and can make demands on the host country. Multinationals pay taxes in the country where they earn profits; however, they can force smaller local businesses to close. Multinationals can learn from their host country in terms of cultures and customs; however, they can pull out of the country at any time, leaving the host country without jobs.

Page 21 Quick Fire Questions

1 For example, health and defence
2 For example, education and leisure
3 The BBC
4 Voluntary organisations are run by volunteers who are interested in the organisation and what it is aiming to do (e.g. Scouts, Guides, local football teams), whereas a charity is interested in raising funds for good causes and has both volunteers and paid employees.
5 Social enterprises are different from other third sector organisations as they are run in a business-like way and have a specific aim (e.g. a social or environmental aim). Their employees get paid in the usual way.

Page 21 Sample Examination Question

1 Organisations in the private sector are owned and controlled by private individuals, whereas organisations in the public sector are collectively owned by everyone, and third sector organisations are not owned by anyone. Private sector organisations aim to make a profit, whereas public sector organisations aim to cover their costs, and third sector organisations aim to raise money for good causes. Private sector organisations raise finance from private individuals, whereas public sector organisations raise finance from taxes, and third sector organisations raise finance from donations, government grants and lottery funding.

Page 25 Quick Fire Questions

1 Objectives are targets or goals that an organisation sets for itself and these are usually expressed in terms of a mission statement. The mission statement will set out how the business intends to achieve these targets and goals.
2 Private sector objectives include making a profit, whereas public sector and third sector are not-for-profit organisations.
3 Businesses may wish to grow in order to increase their market share, to gain economies of scale, and to make sure of their continued survival in the market.

Page 25 Sample Examination questions

1 An organisation can have conflicting objectives as they may aim to make a profit, but also want to keep their customers happy. If customers want low prices, this will conflict with the profit objective.
2 Possible methods of growth for a plc are: vertical integration where two businesses at different stages in the production process merge; horizontal integration where two businesses at the same stage of the production process merge; a merger where two businesses agree to become one; a takeover where one business buys over another; diversification where two businesses in completely different types of production join together; organic growth where a business opens more branches, takes on more employees, etc and grows naturally.

3 Horizontal integration – firms producing the same products combine together. This allows for greater economies of scale, which allows for lower unit costs and increased profits. By becoming larger, they should become better known in the market and this should lead to brand loyalty and increased sales. They might dominate the market due to the greater size of the organisation and can then set prices and encourage customers to purchase from them through large promotional activities. By removing competitors, they will increase sales. Vertical integration – firms at different stages in the production process combine together. This can cut out middle men and allow the organisation to retain all profits made in the chain themselves. Backwards vertical – when a firm combines with a supplier, which ensures that there is constant and consistent supplies of raw materials at appropriate prices. Forwards vertical – when a firm combines with a customer, which ensures that sales are constant and can increase profits. Conglomerate/diversification – when a firm combines with another firm in a completely different market. This means that profits can be made from a variety of markets and sales do not rely on just one industry.

Page 27 Quick Fire Questions

1 Political factors include the government passing new laws regarding health and safety, working conditions or taxation.

2 Economic factors include recession, unemployment, competition.

3 Social changes that influence demand include fashion and taste changes, or changes in population structure (e.g. more old people).

4 Changes in technology include mobile phones, tablet computers, social network sites.

5 A business can become more socially responsible by recycling and caring for the environment.

Page 27 Sample Examination Question

1 Legislation – any new law passed by the government can have an impact on the organisation as they will have to comply with that law, and this usually costs them money. Taxation rates may change, which will affect the profitability of an organisation. The government may introduce new finance schemes for business loans and grants, and this can have a positive effect on business finance. The government may introduce new policies that impact on the business (e.g. education and training for employees).

Page 30 Quick Fire Questions

1 Businesses will find it harder to secure funds for growth.

2 Austerity means that businesses and individuals have less money to spend, therefore there is reduced demand for goods and services.

3 Low interest rates encourages individuals to spend rather than save.

4 It increases economic growth.

Page 30 Sample Examination Question

1 Competition policy can assist and prevent businesses from achieving their objectives, depending on the policy being introduced. The EU allows businesses to achieve growth; however, it can lead to further competition from abroad. Other elements of competition policy prevent businesses from setting high prices, which reduce the amount of profit they can make. Mergers and takeovers can sometimes be blocked by the government, which reduces opportunities for growth.

Page 32 Quick Fire Questions

1 Finance – businesses must have access to the finance they need to run the business properly. Lack of finance can lead to problems. Employees – need to be correctly qualified and trained for the jobs they do, otherwise customers will not be happy. Management – must be able to make good quality decisions on behalf of the business. Existing technology – the business must embrace technology in order to stay competitive.

2 Corporate culture is the overall impression that the business gives to customers and employees. It is about achieving objectives overall.

3 Corporate culture can be achieved by staff wearing uniforms, having a corporate style (e.g. logo, colours, mascot). It can also be achieved by team building activities and good customer service.

Page 32 Sample Examination Question

1 The organisation needs to take into account the ideas/principles of the owners. They need to design appropriate logos, motifs and uniforms. They need to consider a corporate design for shops and outlets. They have to make staff aware of the corporate culture and image, but this can be expensive and may involve staff training costs. The organisation may decide to hold launch events or press conferences. The organisation should have clearly defined policies and procedures.

Page 35 Quick Fire Questions

1 Stakeholders are: employees, managers, owners, customers, government, local community, suppliers and pressure groups.

2 Interdependence of stakeholders means that both sides are prepared to work together and compromise in order to achieve their objectives.

3 Conflict between stakeholders arises when their aims are directly at odds with each other.

4 Conflict between stakeholders may be resolved by the stakeholder with the greatest influence getting their own way, or the stakeholder with the greatest impact getting their own way.

Page 42 Quick Fire Questions

1 A wide span of control is when a manager has a large number of employees under their command, whereas a narrow span of control is when a manger has a small number of employees under their command.

2 Chain of command – where instructions are passed down from one level to another in an organisation. Responsibility – answerable for decisions and actions taken. Delegate – someone requests a task to be done by a subordinate. Functional grouping – grouping by department.

3 A benefit of customer grouping is that goods and services can be targeted directly to the needs of customers in that group.

4 Businesses may group according to city, or council (e.g. East Ayrshire, Morayshire) or by international country (e.g. Italy, France).

Page 42 Sample Examination Questions

1 The effects of increasing a manager's span of control are complex. The manager may experience stress, as the number of employees they are in charge of increases. The manager might feel they do not have enough time to supervise the employees properly. The employees might feel they do not have the proper support from their manager. Employees may resent having to make decisions and may not have the confidence to do so. However, employees may feel more empowered as they will have more tasks delegated to them and they can make their own decisions. Employees may not feel that managers are closely supervising them and this gives them more freedom.

2 Customer grouping can easily build up loyalty. There is a high level of customer care and the organisation can respond to the customer needs quickly. It can be expensive due to high staffing costs to meet customer needs. New staff are needed if there is a new customer grouping or product created. Competition between customer groupings/departments can exist.

3 Staff with similar expertise work together in functional grouping but in product grouping staff are organised around a specific product or service and will have different areas of expertise. The organisation will have functional departments that service the whole organisation, whereas in product grouping each functional area will be responsible for a specific product or service only. In both methods, departments can be more concerned with their own results than the organisation as a whole. Also, departments may compete against each other in both forms of grouping. In product grouping it is easier to identify areas that are performing well, whereas in functional grouping results tend to be for the organisation as a whole. In product grouping each department is more responsive to change, but in functional grouping the organisation can become very large and unresponsive. In functional grouping staff will know exactly who to turn to, but in product grouping this may not be the case. In functional grouping the organisation will have a clear structure, but in product grouping the structure may be less clear and line relationships less clear.

Page 44 Quick Fire Questions

1 Hierarchical structure has many layers of management, whereas flat structure has few layers of management.

2 A matrix structure would be formed for a specific reason, e.g. to work on a particular project.

3 An entrepreneurial structure would be found in smaller oganisations.

4 A centralised structure is associated with a hierarchical structure.

5 A decentralised structure allows decisions to be made across all levels in the organisation, although this tends to be flat structures.

6 A business may wish to restructure to keep with up the changing business environment or to respond to external factors.

7 Delayering is when an organisation removes levels of management, downsizing is when an organisation reduces the scale of its operations across the whole organisation, and outsourcing is when an organisation sends some of its core activities out to another organisation to do on their behalf.

Page 44 Sample Examination Questions

1 In a decentralised structure, decision making is delegated to departments, whereas in a centralised structure, decision making lies with senior managers. A decentralised structure relieves senior managers of a lot of the daily tasks, but in a centralised structure managers carry the whole burden of decision making. In a decentralised structure, subordinates are given responsibility to make decisions (which is motivational), whereas in a centralised structure, subordinates are less motivated as decision making is made only by senior managers. In a decentralised structure, decision making is faster than in a centralised structure, as local managers do not have to consult national managers prior to making a decision. In a centralised structure, procedures tend to be standardised throughout the organisation, but in a decentralised structure, procedures will be decided by local managers. In a centralised structure, decisions are taken for the organisation as a whole, whereas in a decentralised structure, decisions take into account local arrangements/customers. In a centralised structure, a high degree of corporate identity exists, whereas in a decentralised structure, corporate culture is harder to impose.

2 In an entrepreneurial structure, one senior member of staff makes all the important decisions. Decisions are therefore made quickly. Staff are very rarely consulted on decision making. It stifles staff initiative as they are not consulted. The employees know who they are accountable to, but it may place over-reliance on key members of staff.

3 In delayering, a complete level of management is cut out, which will reduce the salaries paid out by the organisation. Managers have an increased span of control, which may result in increased workload for the manager. There may be increased stress for the manager. The staff have to wait to meet with a manager. Communication should be improved and be quicker to pass on, which means the organisation will be more receptive to changes in the marketplace. Empowers the staff, which can lead to increased motivation. However, fewer promotion opportunities for staff could lead to them leaving to gain promotion.

Page 46 Quick Fire Questions

1 Planning – Looking at future needs of the organisation. Organisation – Ensuring necessary resources will be available. Commanding – Instructing others in what needs to be done. Coordinating – Making sure there is joined up thinking. Controlling – Overseeing developments. Delegating – Entrusting tasks to others. Motivating – Encouraging staff to achieve their potential.

2 Strategic – Long-term decisions made by senior management. Tactical – Medium-term decisions made by senior and middle managers. Operational – Everyday decisions that are made by junior managers.

3 Factors that could affect the quality or effectiveness of decisions include: the experience and skills of the manager, the data or information available, the time allowed to make the decisions, the commitment of those who will implement the decisions.

4 Strengths include strong market share, finance available, highly qualified and skilled staff. Weaknesses include out-of-date technology, finance problems, lack of motivated staff.

Page 48 Quick Fire Questions

1 Customer segments are: age, gender, income, social class, cultural, geographical location, education and family lifestyle.

2 Consumer behaviour is influenced by personality, time of year, family events, economic factors, e.g. recession. It is also influenced by routine purchases, e.g. bread and milk.

Page 48 Sample Examination Question

1 Product-led businesses concentrate on their product as they believe the product is good quality and will always sell. They do not undertake extensive market research. However, market-led businesses conduct extensive market research to amend and update their products based on what customers want.

Page 50 Quick Fire Questions

1 Who are the customers? What is their age group? What prices are they willing to pay? This information can be used to improve effectiveness as the business will know exactly who to target and how. They will also be able to set prices accurately.

2 Bias on the part of the interviewer, unreliable information or inaccurate responses.

3 Random sampling, quota sampling, systematic sampling, convenience sampling.

4 When deciding on a sample, the business should take into account the type of product, the location of the business, the stage of the product life cycle.

Page 50 Sample Examination Question

1 Quota sampling involves selecting certain groups of the population that meet certain criteria or market segments, whereas random sampling involves choosing anyone from the population at random. Random sampling gives a good representative of the population as a whole whereas quota sampling is not random.

Page 52 Quick Fire Questions

1 Personal interview, technology survey, consumer panel, hall test, observation.

2 Costs – It is very expensive to carry out as researchers have to be employed. It is very time-consuming to collect. In order to obtain meaningful results, large numbers have to be interviewed. Benefits – The information gathered is relevant. The information is accurate and reliable. The information can be kept private from competitors.

3 Using government data, printed media, e.g. books, journals, online research.

4 Costs – The information may not be relevant to your business. The information may not always be accurate or up-to-date or totally reliable. The information is freely available to competitors so it is not always helpful in gaining a competitive edge. Benefits – The information is relatively cheap to obtain. The information is usually easy to obtain. It is useful for analysing past trends in the market and therefore predicting future trends.

Page 52 Sample Examination Questions

1 Personal interview/questionnaire/survey – This can be done in different ways, e.g. face-to-face on the street, telephone survey, written questionnaire. Technology survey – New technology allows customers to give personal feedback on websites or using mobile phones. Consumer panel/focus group – This is when a group of customers is brought together to discuss a product or service. Hall test – This involves giving a free sample or trial of a product to a group of customers and they are asked to give their opinion once they have tried it out. Observation – A lot of information can be gathered by observing customers.

2 Telephone surveys – used by organisations to call customers and gain their views. Instant feedback can be given. Postal survey – where questionnaires are posted out to customers who complete them and return them to the organisations. Could send these out to all customers, or customers in selected areas, gaining their opinions. Personal interview – where people are stopped in the street and asked questions, it can clarify any questions to aid understanding, and allows two-way communication.

Page 57 Quick Fire Questions

1 Research – This is when research and development of the product takes place. This involves developing a prototype and test marketing in order to get feedback from customers. Introduction – This is when the product is introduced or launched onto the market. Growth – Once customers know about the product, sales begin to grow. Maturity – At this stage everyone who wants the product has already purchased it and sales level out. Saturation – At the very end of the maturity stage, the product is saturated as no further growth is possible. Decline – Sales of the product start to fall as there are no new customers.

2 Any two strategies from the 7Ps – Product, Price, Place, Promotion, People, Process and Physical Evidence.

3 This is when a business has more than one product in their range to sell.

4 Benefits – Customers will already know the existing product lines, therefore new ones can be introduced quickly. Risk of failure is spread across a range of products. Market share can be increased as different products will appeal to different market segments. Disadvantages – If there is a problem with one product, it can affect the reputation of all the products in the line. The business may have to invest heavily in machinery and equipment to make a range of different product lines. The business will continually have to train staff to produce new products in the product line.

5 Virgin, Unilever.

Page 57 Sample Examination Questions

1 Introduction – This is when the product is introduced or launched onto the market. Growth – Once customers know about the product, sales begin to grow. Maturity – At this stage everyone who wants the product has already purchased it and sales level out. Decline – Sales of the product start to fall as there are no new customers.

2 Introduction – Profits are low as there are high outlay costs to get the product onto the market. Growth – profits are increasing. Maturity – profits reach their highest level and start to flatten out. Decline – profits start to decrease.

3 Improve the product – this will attract new consumers to purchase the product. Alter the packaging – this may appeal to a different market segment. Increase/decrease the price – price changes can attract new consumers to purchase the product. Use a different or new advertising campaign/advertising media – this will highlight the product in a different manner. Change the use of the product – new use of the product will be popular with different market segments. Introduce line extensions to the product – various product line extensions will appeal to different segments and may increase overall. Alter the place the product is sold – selling the product in a variety of ways will mean a larger number of consumers can purchase the product.

Page 60 Quick Fire Questions

1 What did it cost to make? What price are competitors charging? Is the product sensitive to very small changes in price?

2 Cost plus pricing is based on the cost of production plus a percentage profit added on.

3 This is when prices are set just below a certain limit, e.g. £19.99 seems cheaper than £20.

4 They use them to compare prices for the same product or service from a range of different suppliers in order to get the best price.

Page 60 Sample Examination Questions

1 Premium Pricing – Choose a high price to sell the product, this will give the customer an image of quality. Market Skimming – Start off with a high price to sell the product. This will appeal to a certain market segment who want the product in the introductory stage. Allows the business to make high profits prior to competitors entering the market.

2 Skimming – price is set high initially when no competition exists, then when competitors enter the market, the price is lowered to market price. Penetration Pricing – price is set slightly lower than competitors to attract customers, and once a customer base has been created, the price is slowly increased to be the same as competitors. Promotional Pricing – a low price is set for a short period of time to boost sales in the short term, possibly even making a loss on the product. Destroyer Pricing – price is set very low compared to competitors, and once there is no competition in the market, the price is then put back up to the previous level or higher.

Page 63 Quick Fire Questions

1 Manufacturer to customer, manufacturer to wholesaler to customer, manufacturer to retailer to customer, manufacturer to wholesaler to retailer to customer.

2 For customers, the bulk is broken down into small amounts; for small businesses, the wholesaler provides discounts.

3 For the customer, a local place to shop with advice and after-sales service; for the manufacturer, a reliable outlet for their products.

Page 63 Sample Examination Questions

1 Retailers are located closer to the customer. They often have an established customer base. They can hold stock. Have trained sales staff who are knowledgeable about the products. Will attract customers by offers of credit facilities. Can offer appropriate after sales services. Retailers buy in bulk. Reduced delivery cost. Retailers pay for advertising. Products displayed attractively by the retailer.

2 Advantages – Saves the manufacturer from making lots of smaller deliveries, so saves on transport costs. Saves the manufacturer from having high stockholding costs as a lot of the stock is held by the wholesaler. If there are changes in trends and fashions, the manufacturer will not be left with unsold stock. Wholesalers can help label and package the product for the manufacturer, which saves time consuming/less work for the manufacturer.
Retailers can buy from wholesalers in smaller amounts, which can help increase overall sales.
Disadvantages – By using wholesalers, manufacturers lose control over the image of their product, which could mean the product not being presented the way the manufacturer would want. Profits are lost to the wholesaler, which could be kept by the manufacturer, improving their financial position.

Page 65 Quick Fire Questions

1 'Into the pipeline' promotions are aimed at retailers and 'out of the pipeline' promotions are aimed at consumers.

Page 69 Quick Fire Questions

1 People, Process and Physical evidence

2 Employees have to be trained to carry out their role properly – the main emphasis is on customer service and customer interaction.

3 Physical state of the building, image of employees, corporate image (e.g. logos, etc), employees in uniform, written policies, etc.

Page 72 Quick Fire Questions

1 Sending emails to customers; asking for replies to certain questions; feedback forms on websites; sending SMS messages; asking for customers to provide ratings; using survey websites such as Survey Monkey.

2 No guarantee that this survey will be read; or technical issues with hardware.

3 E-commerce is the process of buying and selling goods on-line through websites that have customer payment facilities.

Page 72 Sample Examination Question

1 The full range of an organisation's products can be shown on a website; therefore, the products are available for consumers to look at. Customers can purchase online from their own home, which increases sales. It allows worldwide sales in the global economy. Sales can be made 24/7. Reduces costs due to not requiring expensive premises or large amounts of staff. Customers can leave comments on websites. The company can make use of customer details for market research purposes. There is customer satisfaction, with rapid deliveries to their homes and reduced prices.

Page 75 Quick Fire Questions

1 'Just-in-time' stock control means having raw materials delivered as and when they are needed for production.

2 Costs – Suppliers must be reliable for stocks to arrive on time. It can be difficult to respond quickly to changes in demand. Delays in transport or adverse weather conditions can hold up deliveries. Benefits – Avoids warehouse costs or stock room costs, therefore production costs are lower. Avoids deterioration of stock that has not been stored properly. Avoids stocks going out of date or fashion too quickly. Avoids theft or pilfering of stock, therefore improving profit figures.

3 Suppliers must be reliable so that stocks arrive on time. They must be flexible and able to respond quickly to changes in demand.

4 Maximum stock level – This is the highest level of stock that the business will hold in order to minimise costs and make the most efficient use of the space. The level depends on usage and delivery times. Minimum stock level – This is the lowest level that stock should not fall below, in order to make sure that there are no shortages and production does not have to be stopped. The level depends on usage.

5 Warehouse or stock room should be well lit, dry and well ventilated. A system should be used for booking stock in and out of the warehouse. Stock should be used on a first in, first out basis. Accurate records should be kept of stock levels. Warehouses or stock rooms should be supervised and locked. Appropriate space should be given to stock items. All shelves and storage areas should be labelled for easy access.

Page 75 Sample Examination Questions

1 Understocking – Becomes harder to cope with unexpected changes in demand, which means customers may go elsewhere to purchase the product if the firm doesn't have it in stock. If customers go elsewhere, they may lose them completely, and not just the one time. Production may have to stop completely as there are no raw materials to use in production, which can mean paying for workers who aren't producing any goods. Overstocking – Carrying large amounts of stock will increase the cost of storage, reducing profit, and may result in having to pay larger insurance costs. Capital is tied up in stock, which means that the money cannot be used elsewhere, such as advertising. The stock may deteriorate, resulting in larger wastage costs. Changes in trends and fashion will mean that stock might become obsolete and not be able to be sold.

2 Capital is not tied up in stock and can be used elsewhere in the organisation. There is less warehouse space needed for stock. Less stock is stored, which should result in less wastage. Theft will be reduced as stock is more tightly controlled. Changes in fashion or trends will have less of an impact. If stock does not arrive, production can stop. There will be an increase in delivery costs as more frequent transportation exists. There is a high dependence on suppliers.

Page 77 Quick Fire Questions

1 Labour intensive uses mostly humans in the production process; capital intensive uses mostly machines and equipment in the production process.

2 Mechanisation uses machines with people involved; automation is robots and machines doing all the work.

3 Job – piece of furniture or clothing. Batch – bread, cakes, wallpaper. Flow – cars.

4 Advantages – Production costs can be reduced because many products can be made at the same time. There can still be some degree of tailoring the batches to the customer's requirements. Disadvantages – Switching between batches can be time consuming if changes to machinery need to be made. If there is a problem with one product in the batch, the whole batch may be affected.

5 Advantages – Very large numbers of products can be made quickly at the same time, thus lowering unit costs of production. The use of machinery allows the production process to be running constantly (often fully automated). Quality assurance can be built into each stage of the production process. Disadvantages – the product is exactly the same for each customer; there is no tailoring to their requirements. There are very high costs involved for machinery and production lines. There are very few opportunities for employees to use their skills and initiative, as many of the tasks involved are boring and repetitive.

Page 77 Sample Examination Questions

1 Job production – this is usually defined as one 'job' which is done at a time by an individual skilled worker. The job involves a high degree of skill on behalf of the employees and the job can take a long time to complete. Batch production – this is usually defined as groups of products that are made at the same time in batches. Each product in the batch is the same, but there may be slight variations between batches. Flow Production – this is usually defined as very large numbers of products produced continuously on a production line. It is often referred to as 'mass production' or 'line production' as the goods are made on production lines.

2 Job production advantages – The product is made to the specific requirements of the customer. High prices can be charged for the skill and expertise involved. Disadvantages – Can take a long time to produce. Production costs are also high because there are no opportunities for economies of scale to be made.

Page 79 Quick Fire Questions

1 'Quality' usually means a product that has been made using high quality raw materials and highly trained staff.

2 Quality control – This involves checking products after they have been produced to make sure they meet the standards expected. Quality circles – This involves bringing groups of employees together with the management, in order to discuss issues of quality. Employees are usually trained to identify, analyse and solve some of the problems in their work.

3 Everyone in the organisation is trained in quality, and they know how to deliver products and services to customers' requirements.

4 Benchmarking is an approach to quality that involves the business applying a set of standards or benchmarks. The business has to make sure that it achieves these benchmarks in order to stay competitive.

5 Very important and accurate feedback can be received about the customer experience, as employees do not know who the mystery shopper is.

Page 79 Sample Examination Question

1 Quality management systems are as follows. Quality control – This involves checking products after they have been produced to make sure they meet the standards expected. Quality assurance – This involves a planned and systematic approach to checking products at more regular intervals during the production process, and trying to avoid problems happening in the first place. Total quality management – This involves every employee in the organisation ensuring that quality is built in at each and every stage of the production process. Quality standards and symbols – In the UK, there are recognised systems of quality standards (e.g. The BSI (British Standards Institution), which places a Kitemark on products that meet the standard). Benchmarking – Benchmarking is an approach to quality that involves the business applying a set of standards or benchmarks.

Page 81 Quick Fire Questions

1 Fair trade involves giving producers a fair price for their products.

2 Benefits of Fairtrade – Customers are happy to buy Fairtrade products so there will be increased customer loyalty. Most businesses who are licensed for Fairtrade enjoy a good reputation and public image, therefore employees are easier to recruit.

3 Ethical behaviour ensures that products are produced in the right way, e.g. not using child labour, paying good wages, following Health and Safety laws and the Equality Act 2010.

4 Higher prices being charged to customers. Higher prices for raw materials.

5 One benefit of using ethical operations is that customers will have confidence in the business, and therefore sales and profits will increase. Another benefit of ethical operations is employee motivation.

Page 83 Quick Fire Questions

1 Businesses must avoid pollution, dumping of waste and using up limited resources.

2 Recycling helps the environment by allowing waste materials to be reused, also by saving energy and reducing greenhouse gases.

3 Reducing packaging reduces waste and saves on energy. This helps businesses reduce costs, and helps save the environment by using less of the limited resources.

Page 86 Quick Fire Questions

1 Computer Aided Design.

2 Speed, accuracy and continuity and a reduction in the number of employees required, therefore saving costs.

3 EPOS can be used to produce reports on inventory levels that are too high or too low.

4 EPOS can also be used by customers accessing the business website to see if certain items are in stock. They can he held for customers to uplift from the store, or they can be delivered to their homes.

Page 88 Quick Fire Questions

1 Skills analysis of current staff. Forecasting staffing to meet demand. Planning supply of staff.

Page 91 Quick Fire questions

1 Interview, asking candidates to make a presentation, role play, group interviews, team building tasks, assessments or testing.

2 Recruitment is the process of getting potential candidates to apply for the job and usually includes the point of receiving completed applications. Thereafter, selection involves sifting through the applications and selecting candidates to be interviewed or tested.

3 During team building and group discussion activities 'natural leaders' can emerge. Candidates can be assessed on how they interact with others.

4 Personality can be tested by asking about thoughts and feelings, whereas aptitude is tested by literacy, numeracy, problem-solving and reasoning tasks.

5 Group exercises, in-tray exercises, presentations, case studies, psychometric testing, social activities.

6 This is when an employee is taken on for an agreed period of time, so that they can be assessed on their performance during that time. If they are satisfactory, they will usually be kept on.

Page 91 Sample Examination Questions

1 Compare application forms and CVs with the person specification to make sure candidates meet the criteria. Interview the candidates to find out about their personalities and skills. Ask the candidates to take part in presentations, group discussions, role play, etc in order to assess their personalities and skills. Use an assessment centre to test and interview the candidates.

2 Interviews are used to gather information on potential employees' abilities. They allow the organisation to compare candidates in a pressure situation. They give the candidates a chance to respond to questions. The interviewers can compare notes to get a consensus on who the best candidate was. Interview styles can change, allowing the organisation to examine potential candidates under different situations (i.e. long leet and short leet interviews, group interviews, presentations).

3 Attainment – a candidate is given the chance to demonstrate their skills, e.g. it would be used to test skills in ICT or to measure skills against a set standard. Aptitude – assesses a candidate's personal abilities and skills, e.g. it would be used to decide if the candidate had the required skills and aptitude for a job, (i.e. numerical skills for an accounts vacancy). Intelligence/ IQ – measures a candidate's mental ability, e.g. it is used for jobs where candidates may be solving problems. Psychometric/psychological – assesses a candidate's personality and can be used to assess the candidate's mental suitability for a job. Medical – measures a candidate's physical attributes and is used for jobs such as the fire brigade that require certain levels of physical strength.

Page 95 Quick Fire Questions

1 On-the-job, off-the-job and induction training.

2 For example, lectures, role play, job rotation, apprenticeships, multimedia.

3 Higher skilled, more effective employees leads to reductions in customer complaints. Higher skilled, more effective employees leads to reductions in absenteeism and staff turnover. Higher skilled, more effective employees will be ambitious and will apply for vacancies, therefore reducing the skills gap.

Page 95 Sample Examination Questions

1 Staff training allows for a wider pool of skills to be available to the organisation, so staff can carry out a wider range of tasks and cover for absent colleagues. Staff training is motivational for staff and should mean they are happier at their work, which will improve performance. Staff training can improve the quality of product/service provided, which will result in improved customer relations. It improves the image of the organisation, which means they will attract a better calibre of worker and therefore more people wishing to work for them. It should reduce the number of accidents at work, which will reduce any compensation or injuries to employees/customers. It may be required to introduce change and will make the staff more acceptable to change.

2 Costs of staff training are: hiring of 'experts' to deliver the training, costs of hiring venue for training to take place, costs of covering for employees who are away from the workplace, possible lack of continuity with customers when employees are being trained, costs of travel expenses for employees.

Page 97 Quick Fire Questions

1 Maslow's hierarchy of needs; Herzberg's theory of motivators and hygiene factors.

2 A democratic leader consults with employees before making decisions, allows employees to use their initiative and delegates to employees.

3 Rewards help to motivate employees as they feel valued, and if they work harder it will be to their own benefit.

Page 97 Sample Examination Questions

1 Use of staff training to motivate staff. Give bonuses or financial rewards. Make use of profit sharing schemes. Organise team building days or social events. Have staff involvement in works councils/quality circles. Have regular consultation with staff. Job enlargement or enrichment schemes. However, all of these involve time and money, which can result in the business losing profits.

Page 100 Quick Fire Questions

1 Employee relations involves encouraging and motivating staff to develop and perform to their potential in their job. It also involves communicating, negotiating and bargaining with staff on a more official basis through trade unions and works councils.

2 Counselling, stress management, return to work interviews, family friendly policies.

3 Employees will be motivated if they have good facilities and places to relax at work.

4 Appraisals allow employees to focus on working towards pay increases, promotion or training and development.

5 Employees may not perform to their highest level, which affects customers. The business might find it difficult to attract good quality staff.

Page 100 Sample Examination Questions

1 Employees may be set appropriate targets, and staff training could be given in order to allow these targets to be met. Positive feedback could be given to the employee during appraisal meetings. Support systems could be put into place, e.g. counselling. Regular meetings could be held with their line manager or a mentor appointed.

2 De-motivated workforce may result in: decreased productivity, increased staff turnover, increased staff absenteeism, impact on the quality of output, and less co-operation of staff during periods of change could make it harder to introduce new policies or procedures.

Page 104 Quick Fire Questions

1 The purpose of a trade union is to help its members secure the best pay and working conditions possible.

2 Strike – when employees refuse to go to work. Overtime ban – when employees refuse to work extra hours. Sit-in – when employees occupy the building. Work to rule – when employees only do exactly what their contract says. Go slow – when employees still do their job but much more slowly than normal.

3 Employers provide and maintain safety equipment and safe systems of work; ensure materials used are properly stored, handled, used and transported; provide information, training, instruction and supervision; provide a safe place of employment, e.g. fire extinguishers, protective clothing, have health and safety representatives.

4 The equality act bans unfair treatment and helps achieve equal opportunities.

Page 104 Sample Examination Questions

1 The features of the Equality Act 2010 are fair and equal treatment for all employees and removal of discrimination. Potential candidates and existing employees cannot be discriminated on the grounds of: sex, race, marital status, religion, disability, sexual orientation or pregnancy. Employees must be provided with the necessary support to carry out their jobs correctly, e.g. accessible buildings.

2 Strike – when employees refuse to go to work and do not get paid. There has to be a ballot of all members before this can take place. Overtime ban – when employees refuse to work extra hours, which can have a negative effect on customer orders. Sit-in – when employees occupy the building, which prevents normal work from taking place. Work to rule – when employees only do exactly what their contract says and nothing extra. This can damage goodwill with management. Go slow – when employees still do their job but much more slowly than normal, which therefore affects output.

Page 107 Quick Fire Questions

1 A database can be used to store all the personal information details of employees. It can also store salary information, training and personal development information and medical details. This increases efficiency as management can search for specific information quickly e.g. how many employees require training, the total salaries paid to a certain department etc.

Video conferencing can be used for staff training. A group of employees can be trained at the same time in different locations by one trainer. This improves efficiency as the employees do not need to travel and the business does not have to pay for overnight accommodation and travel expenses. Video conferencing can also be used for interviews and employee appraisals and the same advantages apply.

2 Online recruitment websites allow the business to reach a large worldwide audience. Applications can be invited from a wide range of potential employees which means the business can be sure of getting high quality candidates. Online websites allow the business to update advertisements easily and quickly and allows applications to be received quickly. This speeds up the whole recruitment process.

Page 107 Sample Examination Question

Advantages: A wide range of modules can develop a range of skills in employees. The VLE is free for the employee to use and is flexible as training may be accessed by the employees from home. Costs can be saved from hiring expensive trainers.

Disadvantages: The VLE can be expensive to purchase and incurs costs to keep it regularly upgraded. Employees can resist IT and may not carry out the training properly or they might not be as interested or as engaged with the training compared to an experienced trainer carrying out face to face training.

Page 110 Quick Fire Questions

1 Large sums of money can be generated from selling shares.
2 A grant does not have to be paid back whereas a loan does.
3 There is no initial outlay when leasing, whereas buying the asset there is usually a large initial outlay.
4 Debts are sold to a third party who then tries to recoup the debt.

Page 110 Sample Examination Question

1 Bank loan – over a period of time it is paid back (in instalments) with interest, allowing for the payments to be spread out. Bank overdraft – a smaller amount for a shorter period of time borrowed from a bank, it is useful when only needed for a short period of time and is relatively easy to arrange. Grant – might be possible to receive a government grant under certain conditions, it does not have to be paid back. Retained profits from previous years – does not involve any re-payments or interest. Venture capital – provides finance when banks thinks it is too risky – often good for riskier investments or ideas. Mortgage – used to purchase buildings over a long period of time, therefore easy to manage.

Page 112 Quick Fire Questions

1 A cash budget is used to identify periods when cash-flow might be a problem and therefore enable corrective action to be taken.
2 Surplus is a positive closing balance, whereas deficit is a negative closing balance.
3 Increase sales revenue, reduce expenses, spread purchase of assets.
4 Rent, wages, gas, electricity, petrol, etc.

Page 112 Sample Examination Questions

1 Customers being given too long a credit period. Customers being given too high a credit limit. Owners taking out too much money through drawings, and having high debts with increased rates of interest. Suppliers not allowing credit or very short credit period. Sales revenue not high enough. Sudden increase in expenses. Capital expenditure, e.g. purchase of machinery.
2 Use marketing measures to move unwanted stock. Reduce the length of time given to customers to pay for goods. Have a maximum amount owners can withdraw/reduce drawings. Try to get increased credit terms. Find a cheaper supplier. Reduce wages/expenses. Take out a short term overdraft. Increase owners' own capital. Reduce repayment of loans.
3 Cash budgets highlight periods when cash flow will be a problem. They can be used to secure loans or to show investors, and are used to make comparisons between actual expenditure and targeted. They can show periods that the organisation will have cash available for major investment or purchases of fixed assets. They are used to give departments a budget to focus on (targets), and are used to monitor spending throughout the organisation.

Page 117 Quick Fire Questions

1 Income Statement and Statement of Financial Position.

2 Sales less cost of sales.

3 Gross profit less expenses.

4 Wages, electricity, gas, advertising, etc.

Page 117 Sample Examination Question

1 Shareholders could look at any ratios calculated, e.g. gross profit %. Trading account Income Statement shows the profit and loss made from buying and selling stock over a period of time. Shows the overall profit or loss over a specified time period. Statement of Financial Position which shows the financial position of a business at an exact moment in time. Cash budgets show projected income and expenditure for the following year. Share prices show the current value of the organisation.

Page 121 Quick Fire Questions

1 This is bad as it is below the average for the industry. The business will want to find out the reasons why their figure is below average.

2 Increase sales revenue, reduce cost of sales, improve stock management.

3 Increase in the gross profit %, reduction in expenses.

Page 121 Sample Examination Questions

1 The information is historical and the findings do not take into account external factors. New products or product development is not taken into account. Staff morale or turnover is not taken into account, and you can't compare with different organisations, as you do not know the basis used, e.g. stock valuations. It assumes the information they are based on is reliable.

2 Current ratio: current assets/current liabilities, answer of 2:1 is the accepted ratio. Allows managers to monitor liquidity levels of the business and shows the ability to pay short term debts. Acid test ratio: current assets – inventory/current liabilities, 1:1 is the accepted ratio. Allows managers to know that they can pay off debts quickly. Gross profit ratio: gross profit/sales × 100 measures the percentage profit made from buying and selling stock. Can be used by managers to compare to the industry standard. Net profit ratio: net profit/sales × 100 measures the percentage profit after expenses have been paid. Can be used by managers to control expenses or analyse expenses. Rate of inventory turnover: cost of goods sold/average inventory is used to analyse how quickly the stock is sold and is useful for sales of perishable items.

Page 123 Quick Fire Questions

1 Spreadsheets are used to record and calculate accounting transactions. Formulas are used to perform calculations quickly.

2 Graphs can show financial figures at a glance and reveal trends.

3 Costs of purchasing the hardware and software, costs of maintenance and security, technical support and training.

Leckie
the education publisher
for Scotland

Higher BUSINESS MANAGEMENT

For SQA 2019 and beyond

Practice Papers

Derek McInally and Rob Jackson

Contents

ANSWERS Check your answers to the practice test papers online: www.leckieandleckie.co.uk

Introduction to practice papers

This section contains practice exam papers that mirror the actual SQA exam as much as possible. The layout and question level are similar to the actual exam you will sit. This means that you will be familiar with what the exam will look like, so there should be no surprises for you!

Each practice paper has a detailed marking scheme (provided online) that will guide you on how the questions should/could be answered in a way that will maximise the number of marks you can achieve. Each marking scheme also includes hints and tips on how certain questions should be tackled, details of how marks are awarded and advice on what the examiners will be looking for.

How to use this section

This section can be used in two ways:

1. You can complete an entire practice paper as preparation for the final exam. If you want to use the book in this way, you can either complete a practice paper under exam conditions by setting yourself a time limit for each paper and answering it as well as possible without looking at your notes or textbooks. Or, on the other hand, you can answer questions as a revision exercise by using your notes to ensure you produce a model answer. Your teacher/lecturer may mark these for you.

2. You can use the topic index to find all the questions in the book that deal with a specific topic, so that you can revise for end of topic tests and/or assessments. Doing it this way will allow you to focus on areas that you feel you need to work on. If you are part-way through the course, it lets you revise topics that you have previously studied and may help you identify areas you need to work on more.

Command words

In these practice papers and in the exam itself, a number of command words will be used in the questions. These command words are used to show you how you should answer a question. Some words require a longer, more detailed answer than others so it is a good idea to familiarise yourself with the command words as these will help you to answer the actual question that is being asked and will also help you structure your answer more effectively.

Command word	Meaning
Compare	Demonstrate knowledge and understanding of the SIMILARITIES and/or DIFFERENCES between things, methods, ideas or items.
Describe	Provide a statement or structure of characteristics and/or features. More than an outline or list. May refer to a concept, process, situation or facts.
Discuss	Communicate ideas and information on a subject. It may be possible to give both sides of an argument, i.e. give reasons for/against an argument.
Explain	Relate cause and effect and/or make relationships between things clear. Explain answers should have TWO parts – a description of something, then the reason behind it. The IMPACT of what you are talking about must be given to fully answer an EXPLAIN question. In the exam, EXPLAIN answers are often the ones that let learners down. The most common error is that descriptions are given instead of explanations. If you are being asked to explain something, you should be giving reasons for what you are saying. Check your answers to explain questions and make sure that you have used linking words and phrases such as 'because', 'this means that', 'therefore', 'so', 'so that', 'due to', 'since', and 'the reason is'.
Justify	Give reasons for your answer. You should be making an argument FOR the suggestions being made.

Writing in the exam

Before you start writing an answer to a question, assume that the person reading your answer knows nothing. You should explain each answer clearly and in enough detail, but without making it too wordy. Keep to the point and within the scope of the question.

In the exam you should be writing in full sentences (do not give one-word answers) and use proper written English. On the whole, bullet points should be avoided.

Knowing and using the correct business terms and words is crucial to your exam success. It may be a good idea to compile a dictionary of key business terminology as you go through the course. This will be a useful revision tool and will also help you when you sit the exam.

In the exam

Watch your time and pace yourself carefully. Work out roughly how much time you can spend on each answer and try to stick to this. You will have 165 minutes (2 hours 45 minutes) to answer 90 marks. This means you have approximately 1.8 minutes for every 1 mark. (Remember this includes time taken to read the case study and the questions.)

You must answer ALL the questions in Section 1 AND ALL the questions in Section 2.

Section 1, Case study, is worth 30 marks and will consist of a set of mandatory short-answer questions based on the case study. The questions will be drawn from any aspect of the Course and will require you to demonstrate the application of skills, knowledge and understanding within the context of the case study.

Section 2 is worth 60 marks, with all questions MANDATORY.

Questions from each section will be sampled from the Course coverage, ensuring there is no duplication of topics and that there is a balanced coverage across the Course.

These practice papers will help you become familiar with the exam's instructions. It is VERY important that you follow the instructions given on the front of the examination paper, so make sure you read them carefully. When you begin the actual SQA exam, read the instructions carefully in case some things have changed.

Read each question thoroughly before you begin to answer it and make sure you know exactly what the question is asking you to do. (Remember the command words!)

Do not repeat yourself in each answer, as you will not get any more marks for saying the same thing twice. This also applies to diagrams, which will not gain you any more marks if the information is repeated within the written part of your answer. Remember to label any diagrams (e.g. extended product life cycle) carefully and correctly.

Exam practice and revision is the key to exam success. Everyone revises differently so find a way that works for you.

Topic Index

Exam A

Section	Question	1 a	b	c	d	e	f	g	2 a	b	c	3 a	b	c	d	4 a	b	c	d	5 a	b	c	Marks
Management of Marketing & Operations	Technology																						29
	Ethical & environmental										8												
	Quality	4																					
	Methods of production									3													
	Stock management								4														
	Physical evidence																						
	Process																						
	People																						
	Promotion																						
	Place																						
	Price			2																			
	Product				8																		
	Marketing mix																						
	Market research																						
	Customers																						
Management of People & Finance	Technology																			5			32
	Ratios							2															
	Financial statements																					5	
	Cash budgeting																				5		
	Sources of finance																						
	Legislation													4									
	Employee relations											2											
	Motivation & leadership														5								
	Training & development																						
	Recruitment & selection												4										
Understanding Business	Decision making																		3				29
	Structures					3												3					
	Stakeholders																						
	Internal factors		5																				
	External factors						6																
	Objectives																						
	Types of organisation															5							
	Role of business																4						
																							Marks 90

Exam B

		1a	1b	1c	1d	1e	1f	1g	2a	2b	2c	2d	3a	3b	3c	3d	4a	4b	4c	5a	5b	5c	
Management of Marketing & Operations	Technology																			5			
	Ethical & environmental							6															
	Quality																		8				
	Methods of production	3																					
	Stock management																				5		
	Physical evidence																						
	Process																						
	People																						27
	Promotion																						
	Place																						
	Price																						
	Product																						
	Marketing mix																						
	Market research																						
	Customers																						
Management of People & Finance	Technology																						
	Ratios																4						
	Financial statements		4																				
	Cash budgeting																						
	Sources of finance																	3					
	Legislation											5											31
	Employee relations										2												
	Motivation & leadership								4														
	Training & development																					5	
	Recruitment & selection									4													
Understanding Business	Decision making																						
	Structures				4																		
	Stakeholders														2								
	Internal factors															4							
	External factors													5									32
	Objectives			5			3																
	Types of organisation					5																	
	Role of business												4										
	Question	1a	b	c	d	e	f	g	2a	b	c	d	3a	b	c	d	4a	b	c	5a	b	c	Marks 90

Practice Exam A

Practice Papers for SQA Exams

HIGHER
BUSINESS MANAGEMENT
Exam A

Duration – 2 hours and 45 minutes

Total marks – 90

SECTION 1 — 30 marks

Attempt ALL questions.

SECTION 2 — 60 marks

Attempt ALL questions.

In your answer booklet, you must clearly identify the question number you are attempting.

Use **blue** or **black** ink.

It is recommended that you spend 15 minutes reading over the information provided in **SECTION 1** before responding to the questions.

Leckie
the education publisher
for Scotland

SECTION 1 — 30 marks

Read ALL the following information and attempt ALL the questions that follow.

The following information has been taken from the Merlin Entertainments' website and annual report in 2018.

Merlin Entertainments

Our Business

Merlin Entertainments is a global leader in location-based, family entertainment. As Europe's Number 1 and the world's second-largest visitor attraction operator, Merlin now operates over 130 attractions, 20 hotels and 6 holiday villages in 25 countries and across 4 continents. Merlin's purpose is to deliver memorable experiences to its 67 million guests around the world, through its iconic global and local brands, and the commitment and passion of its c.28,000 employees (peak season). The Company invests in the development of outstanding visitor experiences across multiple formats, and consistently achieves above 90% guest satisfaction levels.

Our Passion

We aim to beat our best performance every day. If guests come for their first visit and we 'blow their socks off' then they will return – the challenge is then to keep up that level of performance for their next visit. Merlin delivers unique family experiences through exceptional staff and high quality attractions. Luckily our business is built on LEGO play, fun and imagination, and we'll not run out of that any day soon!

Our Vision

Our vision has been to create a high growth, high return, family entertainment business.

Our Company Culture – The Merlin Way

Our culture is simply 'The Merlin Way' which encapsulates our vision, values and competencies. It is at the heart of what we do. It captures what a Merlin person is about and helps shape how we will continue to achieve business growth and our objectives for the future.

The Merlin Way represents what our company is made of:

- we love what we do
- we care
- we are innovative and fast moving
- we do what we say

- we make every £, $, € ... count
- we take ownership
- For the love of fun!

By applying The Merlin Way to all that we do, we achieve our overall aim – to deliver high quality memorable experiences to customers around the globe.

Our People – Why would you want to work for Merlin?

Our People Strategy is aligned to the business goals and defined by:

1. Employee engagement – we want to attract, retain, celebrate and reward those who share our passion for putting smiles on people's faces
2. Talent and development – we create an environment in which everyone can fulfil their potential and do their best work.
3. Compensation and benefits – rewarding for performance and behaviour that truly embodies our values.
4. Diversity and inclusion – the more diverse the experiences and backgrounds of our people, the more we can offer our customers and the communities in which we work.

To ensure we focus on the areas that will add value to our employees, we conduct an annual survey, The Wizard Wants to Know, which enables us to gain honest feedback from all employees. These results are acted upon and become a key driver of continuous improvements through the engagement of our teams. Engaging with our teams and demonstrating improvement is critical to us.

Product Excellence

Our number one priority is to provide memorable experiences for every guest, from booking to departure, and all delivered within a clean and safe environment.

Product Excellence is our unique function that monitors, measures and analyses the experience of all our guests with the purpose of delivering improvement and creating competitive advantage.

We continually measure our performance via the use of on-site, real-time electronic survey touchscreens and through third party review sites such as TripAdvisor.

Reports and attraction rankings are shared across the organisation to deliver continual improvement. In terms of monitoring feedback, we continue to take complaints very seriously – we engage on social media and have ongoing investment in our attractions to continually refresh the customer experience.

(Source: Adapted from Merlin Entertainments' website 2018 (www.merlinentertainments.biz/)

Further Information

Exhibit 1 — Brands

(Source: Adapted from Merlin Entertainments' Introduction Presentation 2019)

Exhibit 2 — Extract from Merlin Entertainments' Financial Performance 2018

	2018	2017	Change
	£ millions	**£ millions**	**%**
Sales	1,668	1,594	+4.6
Gross Profit	327	323	+1.2
Profit for the Year	234	209	+12

(Source: Adapted from Merlin Entertainments' Annual Report 2018)

Exhibit 3 — Ticket prices for Alton Towers (2019)

Ticket	Price on the day or day before	Price when booked 5 days in advance
Adult	£58	£34
Child	£48	£28.50
Groups 7+	£56	£32

(Source: Adapted from www.altontowers.com/tickets 2019)

MARKS

1. (a) Describe the methods of ensuring quality used by Merlin Entertainments. **4**

(b) Using examples from the case study, discuss the benefits of having a strong corporate culture. **5**

(c) Compare the pricing strategy used by Merlin Entertainments at Alton Towers with penetration pricing. **2**

(d) Merlin Entertainments have a varied product portfolio. Describe the costs and benefits of having a varied product portfolio. **8**

(e) Describe the method of grouping used by Merlin Entertainments. **3**

(f) Explain how external factors could affect Merlin Entertainments. **6**

(g) Describe suitable ratios that could be used to analyse the financial data in Exhibit 2. **2**

MARKS

SECTION 2 — 60 marks

Attempt ALL questions

2. (a) Discuss the use of just-in-time stock control. **4**

(b) Explain the benefits of capital intensive production. **3**

(c) Describe methods an organisation could use to be more environmentally friendly. **8**

3. (a) Describe the purpose of an appraisal. **2**

(b) Justify the use of testing as a method of selection. **4**

(c) Explain the impact of employment legislation on an organisation. **4**

(d) Describe Maslow's motivational theory. **5**

4. (a) Compare the features of a plc with that of an organisation in the public sector. **5**

(b) Describe sectors of industry. **4**

(c) Describe the following terms:

- chain of command
- delegation
- wide span of control. **3**

(d) Compare the types of decision a manager could make. **3**

5. (a) Explain the use of technology by the finance department. **5**

(b) Describe methods of solving cash flow problems. **5**

(c) Describe the purpose of a Statement of Financial Position. **5**

[END OF PRACTICE QUESTION PAPER]

Practice Exam B

Practice Papers for SQA Exams

HIGHER
BUSINESS MANAGEMENT
Exam B

Duration – 2 hours and 45 minutes

Total marks – 90

SECTION 1 — 30 marks

Attempt ALL questions.

SECTION 2 — 60 marks

Attempt ALL questions.

In your answer booklet, you must clearly identify the question number you are attempting.

Use **blue** or **black** ink.

It is recommended that you spend 15 minutes reading over the information provided in **SECTION 1** before responding to the questions.

Leckie
the education publisher for Scotland

SECTION 1 — 30 marks

Read ALL the following information and attempt ALL the questions that follow.

The following information has been taken from the website of H&M.

About Us

Our design team creates sustainable fashion for all, always at the best price. The collections include everything from dazzling party collections to the basics and functional sportswear – for women, men, teenagers and children, and for every season or occasion. In addition to clothes, shoes, bags, jewellery, make up and underwear there is also H&M Home – fashionable interiors for children and adults.

The width and variety of the H&M collections mean customers can always find something to suit their style and their wardrobe. There are H&M stores in 73 markets worldwide, and strong digital presences through 8 clearly defined brands.

H&M designs its own products, has no middlemen, buys the right product from the right market in large volumes, has efficient logistics and is cost conscious in every part of the business. H&M's designers, pattern makers and buyers work in teams to create the collections. Flexible planning of the product range and quick decision making ensure that the collections are continually adapted to what customers want.

Corporate Social Responsibility

Climate change is one of the major challenges of our time. Like many others, we have a keen interest in taking action to tackle this – and also a responsibility to do so. Being 'climate smart' is about making an ongoing series of choices, big and small. For us, that can mean anything from choosing more efficient lighting for our stores, to working with our suppliers to help them reduce their CO2 emissions.

- H&M was the first brand to launch garment-collecting boxes in all stores around the world.
- H&M aim for 100% sustainable cotton in our brands' own assortments by the year 2020.
- H&M group has a commitment to use 100% renewable energy; the share is 96% today.
- H&M aim to ensure the paper-based packaging used do not include fibre sourced from Ancient and Endangered Forests by the end of 2022.
- H&M group has committed to becoming climate positive by 2040. Reducing more greenhouse gas (GHC) emissions than they produce.

Transport, packaging, hangers and shopping bags are all part of the retail business. That said, efficient material use and the application of smart methods to reuse and recycle means we can reduce waste and – one day – get rid of it altogether.

We're committed to reducing, reusing and recycling wherever we can. In our vision of a better fashion future, nothing gets wasted. To achieve this vision, we'll need to inspire everyone who's connected to our business – from our suppliers to our customers – to be a part of the journey.

It breaks our heart to see fashion end up in landfill. So, as the first fashion company in the world, we've launched a global initiative that means customers can hand in unwanted garments – from any brand and in any condition – to H&M stores.

Ethical Behaviour

Fair play, respect and integrity are fundamental to our business. Being ethical also means protecting human rights and providing an inclusive business environment. And not only to take responsibility for our colleagues, but also to serve as a good example wherever we operate.

Our business touches the lives of millions of people around the world. We believe every single one of those interactions should be guided by mutual respect, integrity, transparency and honesty.

When it comes to making ethical business decisions, we are committed to respecting human rights, taking a clear stand against any form of corruption and embracing diversity and inclusion.

- 72% of the employees in positions of responsibility were women in 2018.
- Supplier factories representing 73% of our total product volume has democratically elected worker representation
- H&M Group initiative **Take Care** offers inspiration, guidance and service for prolonging the life of our clothes and reducing waste.

(Source: Copy adapted from H&M's Website 2013, facts and figures updated for 2018 (http://about.hm.com))

Further Information

Exhibit 1 — Extract from H&M's Financial Performance

	Year 2	**Year 1**
	£ (000)	**£ (000)**
Non Current Assets	57,214	50,816
Current Assets	61,576	55,746
TOTAL ASSETS	**118,790**	**106,562**
Current Liabilities	44,219	40,723
Long-Term Liabilities	16,025	6,126
TOTAL LIABILITIES	**60,244**	**46,849**
NET WORTH	**58,546**	**59,713**

(Source: Adapted from H&M Annual Results 2018)

Exhibit 2 — H&M Grouping Information

Distribution of stores by regions (2016)

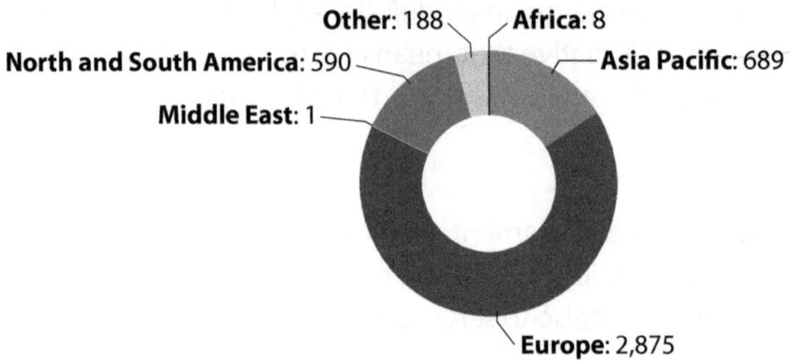

(Source: Adapted from H&M Annual Results 2016)

Exhibit 3 — H&M Timeline

1947
First store opens in Vasteras, Sweden
- Store is called Hennes

1964
First store opens in Norway

1976
First store opens in London, UK

1980–1999
Global expansion takes off
- First stores open in Germany

2000
First stores open in USA and Spain

2004
The 1000th store opens in Lille, France

2006
First store opens in Middle East

2007–2009
First store opens in East Asia

2013
The world's 3000th store opens in Chengdu, China

2018
H&M increase their sales in India with an online presence

(Source: Adapted from H&M website 2013, updated for 2018)

		MARKS
1.	(a) Justify the method of production that H&M would use.	**3**
	(b) Discuss the use of the financial statement shown in Exhibit 1.	**4**
	(c) Describe ways H&M have shown they have good Corporate Social Responsibility.	**5**
	(d) Compare the method of grouping used in Exhibit 2 with product grouping.	**4**
	(e) Discuss the advantages and disadvantages of H&M being a multinational.	**5**
	(f) Describe the method of growth used by H&M.	**3**
	(g) Using examples from the case study, explain the benefits to H&M of operating ethically.	**6**

MARKS

SECTION 2 — 60 marks

Attempt ALL questions

2. (a) Compare two theories of motivation. **4**

(b) Discuss external recruitment. **4**

(c) Describe ways of ensuring good employee relations. **2**

(d) Explain the impact of the Equality Act on an organisation. **5**

3. (a) Compare tall and flat organisation structures. **4**

(b) Explain the impact of government economic policy on an organisation. **5**

(c) Describe the interdependence between the owners and employees of an organisation. **2**

(d) Describe the internal factors that can impact an organisation. **4**

4. (a) Describe how an organisation could improve their liquidity. **4**

(b) Justify sources of finance suitable for a large organisation. **3**

(c) Describe methods of ensuring quality. **8**

5. (a) Discuss the role of technology in the operations department. **5**

(b) Describe factors that would need to be considered when choosing a channel of distribution. **5**

(c) Discuss the use of work-based qualifications. **5**

[END OF PRACTICE QUESTION PAPER]

001/02102019

10 9 8 7 6 5 4 3 2 1

ISBN 9780008365257

Published by
Leckie Ltd
An imprint of HarperCollins*Publishers*
Westerhill Road, Bishopbriggs, Glasgow, G64 2QT
T: 0844 576 8126 F: 0844 576 8131
leckieandleckie@harpercollins.co.uk
www.leckieandleckie.co.uk

Publisher: Sarah Mitchell
Project Managers: Gillian Bowman

Special thanks to
Louise Robb (proofread);
Jouve (layout)

Printed in Italy by Lego, S.P.A.

A CIP Catalogue record for this book is available from the British Library.

Acknowledgements

P14 © Francois Poirier / Shutterstock.com; P16(a) © Jan Faukner / Shutterstock.com; P16(b) © Kzenon / Shutterstock.com; P16(c) © Michael Gordon / Shutterstock.com; P20, BBC - mikecphoto/ Shutterstock.com; P38, Gordon Strachan - Tomasz Bidermann/ Shutterstock.com; P57 © Niki99 / Shutterstock.com; P64, Point of sale - "Easter PoS Display". Licensed under Public domain via Wikimedia Commons - http://commons.wikimedia.org/wiki/ File:Easter_PoS_ Display.JPG#mediaviewer/File:Easter_PoS_Display. JPG; P65, Fergie - Everett Collection/Shutterstock.com; P66, Qantas - Getty Images; P69, Halifax - Bloomberg via Getty Images; P78(a) © TotemArt / Shutterstock.com; P78(b) © Squarelogo / Shutterstock.com; P80, Fairtrade - Thinglass/Shutterstock.com; P101, Industrial action - i4lcocl2/Shutterstock.com; P105(c), P106, P122 (a) © Rawpixel.com / Shutterstock.com; P109, Sold sign - nanka/Shutterstock.com; P122(b) © mama_mia / Shutterstock.com; P122(c) © Atstock Productions; P122(d) © Thamyris Salgueiro / Shutterstock.com;

All other images © Shutterstock.com

The Publishers would like to thank the companies and organisations that have agreed for their logos to be used throughout this publication.

The Publishers would like to thank the following organisations for allowing reuse of their material:

p5 Copyright © Scottish Qualifications Authority
p154-6 © *Merlin Entertainments 2019*
p162-4 © *H&M Group*

Whilst every effort has been made to trace the copyright holders, in cases where this has been unsuccessful, or if any have inadvertently been overlooked, the Publishers would gladly receive any information enabling them to rectify any error or omission at the first opportunity.

ebook

To access the ebook version of this Success Guide visit
www.collins.co.uk/ebooks
and follow the step-by-step instructions.